Susan Gantman

May you

from strength to strength

Stephen

GOSSIP

THE POWER OF THE WORD

GOSSIP

THE POWER OF THE WORD

by

Stephen M. Wylen

KTAV Publishing House, Inc.
Hoboken, New Jersey

Library of Congress Cataloging-in-Publication Data

Wylen, Stephen M., 1952-
Gossip : the power of the tongue : Jewish wisdom for human relations : a self-help book / by Stephen M. Wylen.
p. cm.
ISBN 0-88125-469-X
1. Gossip. 2. Slander. 3. Ethics, Jewish. I. Title.
BJ1535.G6W93 1993
296.3' 85672--dc20 93-24512
CIP

Manufactured in the United States of America
KTAV Publishing House, Inc., 900 Jefferson St., Hoboken, NJ 07030

To the memory of my mother, Maxine Wylen, *z.t.l.*

and (*lehayyim*)

in honor of my father, Joseph Wylen

Contents

Acknowledgments

I would like to thank my wife, Cheryl, for her valuable assistance in the preparation of this work. I am also grateful to other members of my family who gave me advice, assistance, and encouragement, including Eli Wylen, Susan and Ronald Goldenberg, Ruth and David Wasser, and my father, Joseph Wylen and Evelyin Rosen Wylen. I am grateful to the members of Temple Hesed of Scranton for allowing me to serve them and to learn from them and with them how to rise above our human imperfections in the service of God. Thanks to Roseann, Barbara, and many special friends in the congregation who have helped me to arrive at this moment. Thanks and appreciation to the members of the Abington Ecumenical Ministerium.

I am grateful to all my teachers of Torah, including Norman Cohen, Leonard Kravitz, Larry Hoffman, Michael Chernick, Eugene Borowitz, Martin Cohen, David Sperling, Stanley Nash, and many others. Special thanks to librarian Phillip Miller, who sent me off on many wonderful voyages of learning, and whose conversation has always been a stimulant to further study. I am grateful to Rabbi Z. David Levy, who taught me the value of humility and love in the service of our fellow men and women.

Thanks to editor and publisher Bernard Scharfstein for sharing with me the hope that many will benefit from the teachings that are shared in this book.

Chapter 1
Introduction

A fable. All the animals that prey upon humankind gathered in the forest to elect a ruler. The wolf stood up first to announce his candidacy. "Vote for me," said the wolf, "for with my powerful jaws I can rip a person to shreds in no time!"

The lion stood up next. "Vote for me," said the lion, "because with my mighty claws I can cut a person to ribbons just like that!"

Next the snake came forward to claim the crown. When they saw the snake the other animals mocked at him. "Look at you," they all said, "you have no muscles, you can't even stand upright, and yet you ask us to make you our leader?"

Replied the snake, "Have you never heard of the power of a poison tongue?"

When the other animals saw what the snake could accomplish with his venom, they immediately elected him as their ruler.

Malicious speech does great damage to human happiness. It is said that "life and death are in the power of the tongue." This is not just a figure of speech. Idle gossip has been the cause of many needless deaths.

"Sarah" tells everyone in town that a certain local merchant is claiming high quality for goods he knows are shoddy, and furthermore, that his private life makes him the kind of character one would not wish to do business with. The rumors are not true, but so many people believe them that the merchant's business drops off significantly. Distraught at the loss of his livelihood and the destruction of his reputation, the merchant commits suicide.

"Larry" finds out that the wife of an acquaintance of his is having an affair. He knows that his acquaintance has a violent temper, but Larry can't resist the urge to find out what will happen

when the husband finds out, so he tells him. The husband goes home and murders his wife.

In a time of war and military occupation, "Robert" has a little too much to drink in the local tavern. He carelessly lets slip the name of a member of the local resistance movement. An enemy spy is sitting in the tavern, overhearing everything. The next day enemy soldiers kill the resister and his entire family.

Situations like these happen every day. But the misery caused by malicious speech is not limited to the occasional untimely death. Every day, we ourselves and many of the people we know and care about are suffering material loss and emotional damage as a result of malicious speech. It is safe to say that idle and useless gossip is one of the major causes of unnecessary suffering.

There is a children's rhyme, "Sticks and stones may break my bones, but words will never hurt me." Even as they recite it, the children know that it is not true. More often than not, this little rhyme comes out choked with tears. Words can hurt very much indeed. Nor do we become inured to the power of words as we grow older and more mature. Just the contrary, we become more and more aware of the hurtful power of words when they are used as a weapon. Unfortunately, as our awareness grows, so does our own capacity to hurt others with the things we say. Even as we try to build up our defenses against hurtful words, usually without much success, we grow in our capacity and willingness to use words to hurt others. We use backstabbing and gossip to get at our enemies and rivals at work and in our social group. We say nasty things to our spouses, parents, and children as a means of striking out in anger when we do not get our way. The better we know someone, the more we are able to strike through his defenses with words. We do so much damage, then, even to the ones we love the most, because words are a weapon readily at hand and all too easy to use when we lose our self-control.

It is said that one who raises a fist in anger is like one who draws a sword. If you realize that you have acted angrily or in haste, you can lower your fist or return your sword to its sheath, and no harm is done. On the other hand, one who speaks against another person in anger is like one who shoots an arrow. An arrow aimed at someone else cannot be recalled, no matter how much we may regret having shot it.

There is a story of a person who comes to a sage and confesses to him, "I have been guilty of gossiping against my fellow, and now I wish to undo the wrong I have done. Tell me what to do!" Plucking a dandelion that has turned to seed and blowing on it, the sage says, "Go and gather all the seeds from this dandelion, then return to me." "But how shall I gather all the seeds, now that they are scattered to the four winds?" the person asks. Replies the sage, "Now that you have spoken gossip, how shall you recall it, seeing that the rumors you started have been spread by others to every corner of the community? You should have held your tongue to begin with. Nevertheless, go out and try to undo all the damage you have done, and change your ways!"

Most of us like to think of ourselves as good. We do not like to appear evil in our own eyes. Fortunately, we can count on ourselves and on most people not to commit murder or armed robbery. This is hardly sufficient, though, as a definition of human goodness and righteousness. Even though most of us are pretty good, there are wrongs we commit every day that seriously compromise our goodness. If we are religious, we may recognize these wrongs as "sins" against God and humankind. If we are not religious, we may recognize these wrongs as acts which compromise our own expectations of ourselves and impinge upon the right to happiness of others. Most of us go along through life without raising our own awareness of the little things we do each day that hurt others.

There is an old Jewish saying about the sins we commit every day and then excuse to ourselves without thinking too much about them: "Most through petty theft, some through sexual indiscretion, and everyone through the taint of gossip."

Yes, most people commit little thefts every day that they do not charge against themselves. They take an envelope from the office, or accept the accidental return of their coin in a pay phone, or, maybe without even realizing it, pocket the extra change returned to them by a cashier. And yet they continue to think of themselves as good.

Many people find themselves unable to resist the temptation to sexual indiscretion. In all other ways they break no divine law or human trust, and so they forgive themselves the inability to control their passion. They are still "good" people.

There are some men and women so unusually just that they do not commit any ordinary sins. And yet even such saintly people say things every day that contain the "taint" of gossip, in that they could be construed as hurtful to someone else if taken in the wrong way. There is no one, however good, however just, however loving, however strong in faith, who is not guilty of gossip to some degree. Every one of us could grow in goodness by becoming more careful about what we say. Every one of us can benefit by studying the rules of what constitutes gossip and how to avoid it. Since gossip is the most prevalent of all sins, the quickest way to make ourselves better people and the world a better place is to learn to gossip less.

There are many benefits to overcoming the tendency to gossip. Those who refrain from gossip will have many friends and few enemies. They will achieve their objectives more often than gossipers do, without having to engage in needless conflict. They will be admired and praised by others. No one will envy them or wish them bad luck.

Those who are expert at avoiding malicious speech can speak their minds whenever they wish, without making anyone else angry or upset. I urge you to try this simple experiment. Call over a dog that you know well. Speak loving words to it, but in a harsh voice. Most likely the dog will cringe and become defensive. It may run away or growl at you. Now insult the dog with any insulting words that come to mind, but speak in a soft and loving voice. The dog will come to you and ask for more. It will bask in your presence with bright eyes and tongue hanging out.

You may say, well, the dog does not understand English. True enough, but the trick is in realizing that it doesn't make much difference. People are not much different than that dog. You can say anything to them and they will gladly accept your words, as long as you utter them in the right way. Since people understand language, it's just a little more difficult to figure out the right way. If you know that way, you need not hide your true thoughts and feelings or repress yourself in order to get along with others. This is a wonderful benefit that comes to those who learn to control their tongues.

There are two ways to avoid conflicts with others as you go about in pursuit of your own personal goals. One way is to give in to every request and demand that others make upon you. This will enable you to avoid conflict, but you will not acquire self-respect or the respect of others. You will be frustrated in your attempt to meet your own goals. You will not be able to uphold your own principles in the face of conflicting demands.

The other way to avoid conflict is to observe the rules of proper speech. If you do this you will always be able to do what you think best. You will not have to compromise your principles. You will be upright in your own eyes, in the eyes of others, and in the eyes of God. It is worth the trouble to learn the rules that allow you to eat your cake and have it too—to let others come away from you satisfied while you are still able to do things in your own way. This can be done, if you will learn to apply the rules of proper speech.

You may know someone whom everyone loves and respects. In my own work as a rabbi I have run across such people. They are the pillars of their community. They are the ones whom everyone is pleased to honor. They arouse the good instincts of everyone else, causing others to want to be more like them. All such people have one trait in common. They never say a bad word about anyone. Gossip never crosses their lips.

We can't all have great looks or the ability to be funny. We can't all have the talent or charm that makes some people so charismatic. But there is one thing every one of us can do that can make us popular and attractive. We can emulate the most essential trait of those whom others admire most, their love for their fellow human beings. We need only learn to apply the rules of proper speech and then we will be members of this elite group.

You may now be thinking that it is impossible to refrain from improper speech. Or perhaps you feel that gossip is such a pleasant part of life that you are not willing to live without it. Or maybe you object that it is just too overwhelming a task to watch what you say at all times. You would be doomed to failure, so why even try? If such thoughts occur to you, you are not alone. Most people, when they first confront the reality of malicious speech head-on, fall into despair and defensiveness. This is natural. But don't let your worries stop you! Recognize that such concerns are a natural first stage in the learning process, and strengthen yourself to proceed. The results will be worth it.

There are a number of good reasons that we resist changing our patterns of speech for the better. Foremost is guilt. When we study the definition of malicious speech and the rules for avoiding it, we realize that we have committed this terrible wrong many thousands of times in our lives. It is hard to face up to so much guilt all at once—especially since, as was noted above, it is very important to us to think of ourselves as good people.

Guilt is not all bad, when it corresponds to reality and helps us to recognize that we have done wrong and are able to do better. Guilt is easier to bear when we are optimistic about the future. This is easier if we believe in ourselves, in others, and in God. Guilt is bearable if we truly believe in forgiveness. Later we will discuss the importance of granting forgiveness and asking for it. For now, remember that however much you may be guilty of gossiping, you have it within you to change, and you are worthy of being forgiven. Guilt and shame are only temporary, when we are trying our best to improve our ways.

Fear of failure is another reason that we are reluctant to try to control our tendency to engage in malicious speech. The temptation to gossip is so great, the opportunities so many, the illusory reward so immediate, that it is easy to believe we will never be able to completely overcome the tendency to gossip.

In facing fear of failure, it is important to avoid all-or-nothing thinking. We are not faced with the choice of being a complete saint or a habitual gossip. There are many phases in between these extremes. Because gossip is so prevalent, it is hard to eliminate completely. But by the same token, it is easy to make a small improvement. If by attention and hard work you decrease your participation in gossip by only ten percent, you will have accomplished something of enormous worth that will bring untold good to you and to others. Remember also that you do not have to change your ways all at once. If you can refrain from exchanging gossip even once a day, that is a beginning. Later it will become more natural to you to recognize wrongful speech. You will develop instincts that repel you from it. Then you can work to gradually extinguish gossip from your way of life. No one is ever completely free from every hint of wrongful speech, but you can surely succeed in becoming better than average, and that is extremely worthwhile.

Another reason that people are afraid to get started is that they worry over what they will talk about if they eliminate gossip from their conversations. We will discuss this in more detail as we proceed. For now, please have faith that as you learn to avoid malicious speech, topics of greater interest will arise. Admittedly, you will sometimes be dumbstruck and not able to participate in every conversation. Please believe that you will be no worse off for this. You will find that your happiness does not depend on providing the spice to every conversation.

We have mentioned guilt, fear of failure, and worry over what to talk about as three major impediments in the effort to overcome malicious speech. None of these obstacles is insurmountable, if you make the necessary effort.

There is a fourth obstacle to be aware of—the natural perversity of human nature. I have noticed this human tendency at work in the course of my efforts to teach others about gossip. Some time ago I developed a study program on gossip for youth. The students are given a number of real-life situations that arise in the course of their social life. They are asked to make up realistic skits in which they discuss the situations. After learning the rules about how to avoid malicious speech, the students are asked to rewrite their skits without any gossip. I soon learned that the students would always do just the opposite of their instructions in the second set of skits. Rather than try to eliminate all gossip from their discourse, they would use their newfound knowledge to see how *much* gossip they could fit into one conversation. At first I found this behavior upsetting. Once I got used to it, I came to think of it as a normal stage of development. Thinking back, I recalled the same reaction within myself when I first learned the rules of proper speech. For a while, I became a bigger gossip than ever before. Fortunately, this was just a first stage in the learning process. I think this behavior derives from embarrassment and guilt, just as we often make a joke when caught doing something wrong. A truly hateful person could study the rules of gossip with the intention of using them to become more malicious than ever, but for people with a healthy mind this is just a passing phase. As with many illnesses, you have to get worse before you get better.

My first study program on gossip was with a wonderful group of teenagers on a youth retreat. At the conclusion of the program I asked the teens if they would be willing to put into practice what they had just learned. Every one of them declined. "No," they all said, "gossip is too much a part of our lives to do without it. We enjoy gossiping with our friends. We admit that it's wrong, but we are not willing to give up the simple pleasure of gossiping."

A few years later, at another youth retreat, a young woman who had been present at that first session came back from college to see some of her old friends. She told me the following. "Do you remember that study program we did on gossip? Do you remember that none of us were willing to try to live without gossiping? Well, I was one of them, but as time went by I kept thinking about what we had learned, and I felt bad every time I engaged in gossip. I began to concentrate on avoiding gossip. It changed my whole social life for the better. I have many more friends now, and all of them are true friends. My life is much better now because I do not gossip. I want you to know this because I bet it bothered you when we all told you we were not willing to even try to stop gossiping."

The report of this young woman gave me faith in the value of learning to recognize and avoid gossip. Despite initial resistance, many people may come to a happier life, and much harm can be prevented, through the dissemination of this wisdom. You could be one of those who benefit!

My own path to learning about malicious speech and how to avoid it began while I was studying to become a rabbi. I enjoyed looking over the new acquisitions in the seminary's library. Most of the books were scholarly ones with long titles and impenetrable prose. One day a bright blue book with large print and a short title caught my eye. It was called *Guard Your Tongue*, by Zelig Pliskin. I signed out the book, for no other reason but to find out what something readable could be doing in our scholarly library. The book turned out to be an English-language summary, written for Orthodox Jews, of a nineteenth-century Hebrew legal work entitled *Hofetz Haim* ("Lover of Life") by a Lithuanian rabbi, Israel Meir Hacohen Kagan (1838–1933). Rabbi Pliskin's book led me to study the original, which I learned was one of the classics of traditional Jewish legal and ethical writing. The *Hofetz Haim* is a compendium of all the legal sources in the Jewish tradition that deal with forbidden speech. It became so famous that Rabbi Kagan received the highest honor accorded an author in traditional Jewish life—the title of the book became his nickname. Throughout the traditional Jewish world, Rabbi Kagan was referred to as the *Hofetz Haim*, and he is remembered by that name to this day.

The title of the *Hofetz Haim* derives from a verse in the Book of Psalms. "Who is the one who loves life, whose desire is for years of good fortune? Guard your tongue from evil, your lips from deceitful speech. Shun evil and do good, seek peace and pursue it" (Psalm 34:13–15).

My discovery of the *Hofetz Haim* and the laws of forbidden speech opened up a whole new world to me. I was immediately impressed by the wisdom of these rules and their obvious application to my daily life. Following Rabbi Kagan's advice, I regularly reviewed the main rules and returned periodically to restudy his book. I became aware of how often I engaged in improper speech, and I embarked on a venture to improve myself. It proved incredibly difficult, and sometimes I went backwards instead of forwards. I still go through periods when I lapse and engage in forbidden speech. It was only a short time, though, before I began to see some changes in myself. I quickly began to experience the positive results. Not only was I getting along better with others, but I found it a lot easier to live with myself. Even when I caught myself gossiping, I took satisfaction in knowing that at least I was trying to improve.

The result of my own efforts has been enormously gratifying and very helpful in my chosen life as the religious leader of a congregation. I have kept old friends and acquired new ones, and have deepened the friendships that mean the most to me. Because of my work I come into contact with many people and work with them on many projects. Often I must do things that I know will displease others. Sometimes I must turn down earnest and heartfelt requests. Inevitably, some people become angry with me, even furious. Yet to my knowledge I have never made a long-term enemy in my years as a rabbi. When someone becomes my enemy I am able to continue loving that person, confident that before too long he or she will once again be my friend and good co-worker. All of this is possible because I study and practice the rules against forbidden speech.

The laws of forbidden speech are a jewel in the crown of the Jewish legal-ethical system. They demonstrate convincingly that the body of law derived from Scripture is not "dry and arid legalism," as unlearned critics have so unjustly accused. The laws of forbidden speech breathe with life, spirituality, and the will to ethical living. They demonstrate understanding and compassion for the human condition. I live a modernistic path of Judaism that has rejected Jewish traditional law (called *halakha* in Hebrew) as the basis of religious life. Though I do not live by the law, I have come to see, through my study of the *Hofetz Haim*, that it provides a firm foundation for a modern religious or humanistic ethical system. Without a foundation in absolutes, such as the traditional law codified in the *halakha*, our ethics are in danger of becoming mere self-justification. This has happened for too many of us in modern society. The law gives us a way to be good and a reason to be good.

I think it is no accident that laws and rules guiding permitted and forbidden speech should arise especially within Judaism. There is a teaching that "every virtue has its corresponding vice." This is an important teaching, because it reminds us that we do not grow into virtue all at once. By the very effort to grow in virtue we develop within ourselves certain vices that, in turn, will require effort from us to overcome. We must always strive for balance.

The ability to engage in verbal debate with acuity and wit is a virtue that was highly prized in traditional Jewish society. This follows the Jewish teaching that the will of God is revealed through the debates of scholars. Speech was highly prized in the Jewish world; silence in a group of Jews was unheard of. The vice which corresponds to such verbal acuity is the capacity to tear down others. The Jewish tradition warns against the scholar who uses his knowledge, reason, and wit only to tear down and not to build up, to embarrass and ridicule others rather than build up our understanding of God's revelation. The laws, rules, and teachings about malicious speech were developed to curb this vice, which could otherwise be a plague to a highly verbal society.

Jewish law defines two major categories of forbidden speech. One is called *lashon hara*, the other, *rekhilut*. Literally, *lashon hara* means "the wicked tongue," while *rekhilut* means "merchandising." In Jewish legal usage, *lashon hara* refers to things it is forbidden to say, while *rekhilut* is the practice of repeating those things to others. *Lashon hara* is malicious speech; *rekhilut* is talebearing. The most common form of *lashon hara* is gossip, though the term *lashon hara* is much broader than the English word "gossip." It is more accurately translated as "malicious speech," but for convenience' sake we will use the simpler term "gossip." From this point on, the word "gossip" in this book refers to all forms of forbidden speech that are included in the category of *lashon hara*.

Rabbi Kagan, the author of the *Hofetz Haim*, lived in the Baltic state of Lithuania. In his time Lithuania was a world center of traditional Jewish scholarship. Its capital city, Vilna, was called the Jerusalem of the North. Lithuania boasted of many fine yeshivas, the academies of higher Jewish learning where future rabbis were trained in Jewish law and the interpretation of sacred texts. Yeshiva students concentrated their study on the Talmud, the great sixth-century compendium of the legal debates of the ancient Jewish sages. The common method of study was called *pilpul* ("pepper"), the minute analysis of texts to resolve all contradictions within them. *Pilpul* is similar to the scholastic method of medieval Christian scholars.

In the late eighteenth and early nineteenth centuries the Hasidic movement created a great challenge for the yeshiva world. Hasidism was a mystical, revivalist movement. Hasidic Jews favored fervent worship and joyous, divinely directed living over the coldly intellectual world of the yeshiva. Hasidic Jews resented the haughty superiority of the scholars. They did not find any uplift in rabbinic sermonizing on minutiae of the law. In southern Poland, particularly, the Hasidic movement took off. The charismatic "rebbe" replaced the learned Talmud scholar as leader of the Jewish community.

The yeshiva remained strong in the north, in Lithuania, but it was clear that educational reform was in order. The yeshiva had to become more responsive to the daily requirements and spiritual needs of ordinary human life.

Rabbi Israel Salanter (1810–1883) shaped one of the greatest responses to this need, the Musar movement. The Hebrew word *musar* means "ethics." Rabbi Salanter developed a curriculum in ethics to accompany the traditional Talmud curriculum of the yeshiva. This effort was contemporary with, and comparable to, Dewey's attempts in America to replace the irrelevant Classical education in American schools with a more practical education intended to generate productive citizens. But unlike Dewey, Salanter was more interested in the ethical conduct of his students than in their eventual ability to gain a livelihood from their learning.

The students at the Musar yeshiva studied several historic Jewish guidebooks to holy and ethical living, several of which were written under the influence of Jewish mysticism and Messianic expectations. These included *Duties of the Heart* by Rabbi Bahya ibn Pakuda, *Path of the Upright* by Moses Haim Luzzatto, and *Gates of Repentance* by Rabbi Jonah Gerondi. These texts attempted to delineate in legal prescription and biblical interpretation the spiritual and ethical demands that Judaism makes upon the heart and soul of the believer.

In addition to the study of ethical texts there was the *musar shmooze*, or "ethical discussion." Rabbi Salanter would talk for hours on end about the need to live an ethical life. His followers continued this system of haranguing their students. Salanter believed that at least something of whatever words enter a student's ear goes into the memory and becomes an aspect of personality. The hours of *musar shmooze* would eventually wear away a person's evil desires and train the soul to yearn for the good.

Musar students conducted social experiments intended to inure them to social pressure. Like the "Just Say No!" campaign intended to keep young people off drugs, the idea of these experiments was to keep the young from being lured into sinful ways by their more reprehensible peers. The Musar students would go about the streets dressed for the wrong season of the year and act in other intentionally strange ways so that they would become used to hearing and ignoring the mockery of others. A truly good person must care nothing for the opinions of others, and must be concerned only to be right at all times in the eyes of God.

The lofty goal of the Musar movement was to create an ethically perfect human being. Rabbi Salanter and his followers attempted to resolve one of the most difficult ethical dilemmas. A good person acts selflessly. A bad person acts selfishly. Since a good person takes pleasure in doing good, can we say that the good person is inherently any better than the bad person, or is he just blessed with a more acceptable set of desires? The highest level of ethical living is to do good disinterestedly, just because it is good. But how can we reach this level, when the more good we become, the more pleasure we take in doing good?

The Musar response to this dilemma was to train people to do good without taking any pleasure in it. In order to do this the students had to squelch the instinct that derives pleasure from doing good. Without this instinct, how was one to know if one was doing right or wrong? One certainly could not rely on feelings in this case. The response of the Musarniks was to study in the greatest detail the laws of right and wrong behavior. They were then able to make ethical decisions rationally, on the basis of knowledge alone, without recourse to feelings that could cheapen the ethical value of a deed.

It was in this atmosphere that Rabbi Kagan wrote his book on the laws of proper speech. By thoroughly learning the laws set forth in the *Hofetz Haim* and applying them diligently, one could become perfect in speech, knowing the right words for any situation, no matter how complex or ambiguous. Rabbi

Kagan himself was a renowned leader of Lithuanian Jewry, deeply involved in communal affairs in times of great stress and strife. Despite this, he was never heard to speak even one single improper word in his whole life.

When the *Hofetz Haim* grew old he became rather deaf. He considered this not a handicap but a benefit. He used to say, "Knowing how I felt about gossip, the more brazen people might have tried to whisper it to me, but no one would dare to shout gossip in my presence."

The Musar movement did not last long as an organized movement. Its demands upon the human being were too great to be borne. Many graduates of the Musar yeshiva became overly severe and joyless in their approach to life. This often created more harm than good for those who had to live with them. But even if the Musar movement was rather extreme, its good intentions led to some excellent and lasting reforms in Jewish education. The Musar movement made some significant contributions to the human endeavor to live ethically. Rabbi Kagan's work on proper and forbidden speech has lasting significance.

The *Hofetz Haim* as written would not be of much interest to anyone but an Orthodox Jew, and not only because it is written in Hebrew. The book is full of the legal terminology and cultural assumptions of traditional Jewish life. The *Hofetz Haim* presumes a life situation like that of traditional Jews in the Lithuania of the past century—a persecuted minority living under an oppressive government and gravely threatened by political and social modernization. This was a community that suffered repeated massacres at the hands of extremists of both Right and Left until nearly all its members were murdered by the Nazis. The remnants of the culture were then wiped out by Stalinism.

To be useful to us today, the teachings of the *Hofetz Haim* must be universalized. In our society we presume equal rights for all minorities, even if we do not always live up to this ideal in practice. We live in a democracy. We can generally presume that we are living by just laws and that all citizens can receive justice from the courts. We have a global view of human society that encourages us to appreciate the distinctions between different faiths and cultures.

Rabbi Kagan was deeply concerned about sectarianism. Many Jews in his day were abandoning the old ways as the traditional Jewish world came under pressure from the forces of modernity. In the *Hofetz Haim* he taught that it was a good deed to speak against such people and make them into a negative example for others. In our own open society I do not believe that we can justify the public condemnation of "heretics" and "sectarians." On the contrary, I believe that we must extend to everyone that respect which Jewish law originally extended only to those who accepted its authority and lived by it.

For these reasons, I do not claim that the teachings which follow in this book always agree with those of Rabbi Kagan as written in the *Hofetz Haim*. They are inspired by him, but where I believe it is necessary to follow a different path I have granted myself that freedom. In addition, ever since the *Hofetz Haim* made me aware of the imperative to watch my speech, I have watched and listened closely for other wise teachings that are useful in this endeavor. I include in this book rules that are not mentioned by the *Hofetz Haim* but which I have collected through my own life experiences. Also, many of the rules receive their primary inspiration from other sources, Jewish and non-Jewish. As we are taught: "Who is wise? One who learns from every person" (Avot 4:1).

There are many books of psychology and self-help that claim to teach the way to a better, happier, and more productive life. Sadly, these books often teach us how to be insincere, to fake interest in others for the sake of our own advancement. The worst books of popular psychology teach superficiality and a selfish and self-defeating disregard for standards of right and wrong. In the long run it is not possible to succeed in life by concentrating only on ourselves and our own needs.

By being careful about what you say you can maintain complete personal integrity while acquiring the influence with others that you need to meet your life goals. The key to human happiness does not lie in the unconscious mind, nor in the sex organs, nor in the heart, nor in any organ of the human body other than the tongue. It is said that God made every other organ and limb of the body upright, but made the tongue lying down and encased in four walls, to teach us that if we control this organ we shall be master of them all. If we become wise in knowing when to speak and when to keep silent, what to say and how to say it, then everything truly desirable in life will be ours. We shall approach ever closer to that happiness which is our ultimate goal. We shall truly be "lovers of life."

A story is told of the sage Gamaliel and his wise servant Toby. One of the tasks of the sage was to inspect the marketplace to ensure the quality of the produce sold there. One day Gamaliel was very busy and did not have time to go down and inspect the market. He sent Toby to the market with instructions to purchase the worst thing he saw and the best thing he saw and bring them back.

Toby went out and returned a while later.

"Show me the worst thing in the marketplace," said Gamaliel, and Toby laid down a piece of tongue that he had purchased.

"Show me the best thing in the marketplace," said Gamaliel, and Toby laid out another piece of tongue. Gamaliel looked closely but could see no difference between the two pieces.

"What is the meaning of this?" asked Gamaliel. "I sent you to bring me the worst and the best, but you bring me two identical tongues."

Toby said, "Nothing is worse than the tongue when it speaks words of gossip, and nothing is better than the tongue when it speaks words of kindness."

And Gamaliel praised Toby for his wisdom.

Chapter 2
Gossip and Talebearing

> Gossip kills three people at once: the one who speaks it, the one who listens, and the one about whom they speak.
>
> —Numbers Rabba 19:2

GOSSIP DEFINED

In this book we use the term "gossip" in the specific sense of any malicious statement about another person. In Jewish tradition such statements are called *lashon hara*—literally, "the evil tongue." *Lashon hara* is any statement about someone that lowers him or her in the esteem of the listener.

Reuben says to Rachel, "Have you noticed that Janice doesn't have much variety in her wardrobe? She wears the same things all the time."

Sarah says to Sam, "Robert is one of the dumbest kids in our class."

Lewis says to Laura, "I wouldn't trust Richard behind my back for even one second."

All of the above statements are gossip, and would be better not said. All have the effect of making the listener think less of the person under discussion. Gossip may be about someone's morals, taste, actions, or character. Gossip may refer to any aspect of the person who is its subject. Whether the statement pertains to something essential or something incidental, it is gossip so long as it lowers the subject in the esteem of those who hear it.

"Matthew cheats at cards. And I'm not gossiping when I say this; it's absolutely true."

The person who made the preceding statement mistakenly believes that a derogatory statement about someone else is not gossip if it is true. In our definition of gossip we do not distinguish between true and false statements.

In a sense it is precisely the truth of a disparaging statement about another person that makes it gossip. If the statement is false it is slander, which is even worse than gossip. Slander, the deliberate spreading of false information to damage another person's reputation, can be cause for a civil suit in a court of law. Even unintentional slander, when one mistakenly thinks one is repeating true information, is a very serious offense. If you are absolutely sure that the damaging information you know about someone else is true, that is not an excuse to repeat it. The very essence of gossip as opposed to slander is the fact that the information is true, but damaging. It is better to not say anything about another person, true or false, which makes the listener think less of that person.

GOSSIP ABOUT FRIENDS

It makes no difference whether the subject of a derogatory statement is an enemy or a friend of either the speaker or the listener. One might think it is acceptable to repeat gossip about a friend, since a friend is protected by your love from the negative consequences of gossip. It is still gossip if it will make the listener think less of the person under discussion, even if only temporarily.

Lindsay and Jennifer are best friends. One day they get into a little argument about where to go shopping, and they part company in anger. When she gets home Jennifer says to her husband, "I love Lindsay like a sister, but sometimes she can be awfully stubborn."

In this case, Jennifer is guilty of gossiping. It does not matter that Lindsay is her friend, and that Jennifer feels love for her even as she voices her complaint. Jennifer's complaint is still aimed at making her husband think less of Lindsay at this moment.

John has an argument with Fred. Later that day he runs into Fred's best friend, Rick. John says to him, "Rick, nobody knows Fred better than you. Tell me, how do you handle it when Fred is wrong and just won't admit it?"

In this case, the speaker is confident that no matter what he says about his subject, the listener will still feel friendship for him, since they are best friends. Even so, John should not speak negatively about Fred, because it might cause Rick to think less of his dear friend during the discussion. Rick might have cause to say to himself, "Yes, I like Fred a lot, but John is right—he can be awfully pig-headed."

The truth of a statement is not relevant to the question of whether it is acceptable or gossip. The feelings of the speaker or the listener toward the subject are not relevant. The only thing that matters is the *effect* of a statement upon the listener. Before saying anything about another person, one should always ask oneself:

"What will be the effect of what I am about to say on the people I am speaking with?"

If the effect will be a negative opinion of another person, then it is better to keep silent.

POSSESSIONS

Just as one should not speak negatively about anyone else, so too one should not belittle another person's possessions.

"Jeremy's car is really an old clunker!"

"Maria's clothes are all last year's fashions."

"Al and Roberta's house is the least valuable one on their block."

People's possessions are dear to them. Many of us feel that our property is an extension of ourselves or a statement about who we are. To disparage someone's possessions, then, is in a sense to disparage the owner of the possessions. It is especially wrong to gratuitously disparage a merchant's goods, since his or her very livelihood is at stake.

"Oh, are you shopping for carpet at Johnson's? What a schlock merchant!"

"Don't tell me you're thinking about buying your used car from A-One! They've got nothing but lemons on their lot!"

Later we shall discuss the obligation to warn others against being taken in by dishonest merchants. That is a different matter than tossing out an offhand comment, simply for the pleasure of it, that disparages all the merchandise in a shop. This is particularly so if one is speaking of the wares of a business competitor, for then the intent is surely malicious.

EXCUSES FOR GOSSIP

Terry says to his friends, "Did you hear that Theresa was arrested for shoplifting? I'm not repeating anything new; it was in yesterday's newspaper."

Suzanne says to Rebecca, "I did poorly on the test myself, but Liz really messed up. She doesn't know anything!"

Brian says to Jeff, "That guy Jim is a slimy character. And I'm not talking behind anybody's back. I would say the same thing to his face if he were here at this moment."

The speakers in the above situations know that they are gossiping, but they believe that they have acceptable excuses for engaging in the forbidden pleasure of gossip. Hopefully, they will someday learn that there is no excuse for gossip.

We have seen that speaking the truth is not an excuse for gossip. Nor is love for the subject of gossip an excuse. Let us look at some other common excuses.

Sometimes we think that it is acceptable to repeat gossip if it is common knowledge. If something has already been printed in newspapers and magazines, or if everybody is already saying bad things about a certain person, what additional harm could come from repeating the details?

It is better not to repeat gossip even if it is common knowledge. The person to whom you are repeating the gossip may not have heard it before, and then you would be guilty of spreading gossip. Also, your listeners may consider you to be a more reliable source than the newspapers or the local grapevine. In this case, you would reinforce the gossip by repeating it, and perhaps move people from doubt to certainty about the truth of the rumor. Even if all your listeners have heard the story and you are not giving them any new information, by repeating common gossip you are accustoming yourself to engaging in this kind of speech. Moreover, the subject will feel even more hurt on learning that you are repeating the gossip.

"It's bad enough that I have to see my name in the papers. Do I also have to be a subject of discussion for all my so-called friends?"

Please do not impose this extra indignity on your acquaintances. When our misdeeds become common knowledge, that is when we are most in need of true friends—friends who do not gossip about us.

Many people excuse their gossip by including themselves in their disparaging statements. Including yourself in no way lessens the damaging effect of critical comments about others. By including yourself you have gossiped against two people—someone else and yourself. It is better not to gossip against yourself even if you do not include others in your statements. You deserve to be treated with the same dignity as everyone else. Suicide is illegal because our obligation to protect life extends to our own person. Similarly, the ethical rules that apply to our treatment of others apply also to ourselves. Self-deprecation is not humility. True humility requires us to grant honor to ourselves as human beings, creatures in the divine image. If we think poorly of ourselves we may try to bring others down to our level by gossiping against them. If we respect ourselves we are more likely to show respect to others. For our own sake as well as for the sake of others, we should not try to excuse gossip by including ourselves in unfavorable comments.

Mrs. Jones, you are a serious candidate for this job. Your resume is very impressive. We are looking to hire a person who can be honest with herself. Tell us, Mrs. Jones, what do you consider to be your worst faults?"

"I'm sorry, Mrs. Smith, but I cannot speak badly of anyone. Would you like to know about the personal goals I have set for myself this year?"

Gossip is still gossip, whether the subject is present or absent when it is spoken, whether it is spoken openly or in secret. It is gossip if it lowers the subject in the esteem of the listener, even if you would be willing for the subject to know what you are saying.

The damage done by gossip is not decreased if the speaker tries to make it humorous rather than malicious in tone. Sometimes we try to excuse our gossip by turning it into a joke. It is all the same whether you spoke seriously or in jest. The desire to be funny is not an excuse for gossip.

Ivan hears that Jim has been telling people what an air-head he is. He confronts Jim about this. Jim replies, "Well, yes, I did say some things about you, but I didn't really mean them. Everyone was joking around, and they all understood that I was just being funny. You do have a sense of humor, Ivan, don't you?"

SUBTLE GOSSIP

Most people know in their hearts that gossip is wrong. Often, when we are gossiping, we try to soften the impact of what we are saying—or the judgment against ourselves as gossipers—by being subtle. Perhaps we compliment someone but roll our eyes as we speak. Perhaps we make a gesture with hand or face when someone's name comes up. Perhaps we speak well of someone else but do so in an ironic tone of voice to signal disapproval. Signaling a derogatory intent when speaking well of another person is the same as speaking gossip openly. (Warning to the deaf: Your disability does not prevent you from engaging in gossip. On the contrary, you must be extra cautious about the many subtle means of gossiping which are uniquely at your disposal!)

"Everyone in school thinks Mr. Halperin should be teacher-of-the-year," James says to his friends, as he rolls his eyes and makes an obscene gesture with his hand. Everyone laughs.

"Well," says Roberta in her most droll voice, "this chairmanship is just right for Betty." There are giggles all around; everyone knows that Betty is not a good organizer.

Gossip can be in writing as well as in speech. It is gossip to write something defamatory about another person and then publish it, show it to others, or leave it where it might be found and read. It is equally wrong to show others a piece of correspondence addressed to you if that will cause the readers to think worse of the writer. This could happen if the penmanship and spelling were poor or if the letter was poorly written, displaying the writer's ignorance or limitations. One should not show others a letter that contains embarrassing confessions.

Jamie is very angry with her mother. She writes all kinds of nasty things about her in her diary. Instead of closing the diary and putting it in her drawer, as usual, she leaves it open on her desk. Her mother notices the diary when she is straightening up the room. She can't help but see all the hurtful things that Jamie has written about her.

Bret writes a love note to Amanda. Bret is not very good at romance, or writing. His note is full of overblown metaphors and silly professions of affection. Amanda shows Bret's letter to her girlfriends, and they all have a good laugh.

LISTENING TO GOSSIP

If it is tempting to talk about other people, it is even more tempting to listen in when someone else has a juicy piece of gossip. Many people who would not be the authors of gossip believe there is nothing wrong with listening to gossip. Speaking is active; listening is passive. Let the burden be on the head of the speaker! The general rule about listening to gossip is this: *Listening to gossip is the same as speaking it.*

If you willingly listen to gossip, you are as responsible as the speaker for the negative consequences. In some ways it is even worse to listen to gossip than to speak it. By providing an eager audience you encourage the speaker to go on. In addition to having participated in gossip, you are then guilty of leading another person astray.

There are cases, however, where it is necessary to listen to gossip. You may listen if you have a material need to hear what is being said—for instance, if someone is warning you that another person intends to do you harm. We shall discuss such special cases later on. In most instances, though, it is better to close one's ears to gossip.

If someone is about to speak gossip in your presence, you may interrupt to ask if it is truly necessary for you to hear this derogatory information.

"Jane!" Samantha shouts as she comes running up. "Wait till I tell you what I just saw Molly doing!"

"Hold on," says Jane. "Is there any reason that I have to know this?"

"Well," says Samantha, "I would think you would want to know what your friends are up to."

"You know what?" says Jane. "Really, I don't think I have any need to hear what Molly did, but thanks anyway. Tell me about something else. How are you doing these days?"

It is always acceptable to listen to gossip if your only intention is to correct the misimpression created by the speaker.

Dylan listens patiently as Mark tells everyone how Jason neglected to buy him a present even though he came to Mark's birthday party. When Mark is done speaking, Dylan informs him and everyone else that Jason recently suffered a business loss, but was so unassuming that he didn't want to burden other people with his troubles. Blushing, Mark confesses, "I guess there was a good reason after all that Jason didn't buy me a present. It was nice of him to come to my party and act cheerful for my benefit."

In this case Dylan did the right thing by listening to the gossip, since he was able to correct the wrong impressions it created.

TO PREVENT HEARING GOSSIP

If people begin to gossip in your presence, try the following strategies:

1. Quickly change the subject.
2. If that does not work, politely ask the speakers to stop gossiping.
3. If that does not work, or you cannot speak out, walk away.
4. If the speakers will not stop and you cannot remove yourself from the premises, put your fingers in your ears and make noise so as not to hear what they are saying. If you are afraid of appearing foolish, put a look of steely disdain on your face and do nothing to encourage the gossip. Remember: It is better to appear foolish in the eyes of other people all your life than to appear wrong in the eyes of God for even one moment.

George is in a car with some of his co-workers when they begin to speak disparagingly about a person who works in their office.

"Hey, guys!" George says, "Did you see the football game on TV last night? I can't believe the Giants won, can you?" The guys ignore George and continue their conversation.

"Look," says George, "I'm really not comfortable with this discussion. We shouldn't be talking about someone else like this, especially a co-worker."

"Come off it, George," says the driver. "What makes you so sensitive?" The conversation continues.

George doesn't dare make a scene in front of his co-workers, so he puts on a blank stare and tries to remember the words to old Beatles songs so that he doesn't hear what is being said.

If you are forced against your will to listen to gossip or if a word of gossip arises inadvertently in a conversation, try not to believe what you have heard. If there is no doubt regarding the facts, tell yourself that there is probably some extenuating circumstance of which the gossipers are not aware. The matter may not be as bad as it sounds, or it may be more forgivable than it seems. If there is no doubt about the facts or the interpretation, then at least resolve in your heart to take no pleasure from hearing gossip about another person.

"Guess what!" Ed says to Reuben. "I saw Bill peeking into his math book during the exam. Lots of others saw it, too. Everyone knows now that Bill was cheating on the test."

Reuben does not like to hear gossip, but he has to admit to himself after Ed's words that Bill must have cheated on the test. Reuben reviews to himself all the reasons he can think of that might lessen Bill's culpability. Maybe Bill had studied, but hadn't gotten any sleep the night before the exam because of a family problem. Because Reuben has accustomed himself to dislike gossip, he is displeased to have heard bad news about Bill, even though Bill is not one of his favorite people.

If you accustom yourself not to eavesdrop on conversations, even when people are speaking openly within your earshot, you can prevent yourself from inadvertently hearing much gossip.

"Sarah, I can't believe you were sitting right around the corner from us. Please, don't pay any attention to what we were saying about Ellen."

"About Ellen? What! I didn't hear a word you two said."

"Oh, thank goodness. Forget I ever mentioned it!"

You may listen to gossip if the speaker is bursting with anger and quite obviously determined to tell someone. Better you than someone else, since you are not a habitual gossiper. You know that you will not believe the gossip and will not repeat it to anyone else. This provision applies when you are sure that you will be able to calm the speaker down, so that the tale will not be repeated to someone else.

Jill comes up to Lisa, mumbling under her breath about Rose. "What's the matter?" asks Lisa. "You look upset."

"It's that Rose!" says Jill. "You should hear what she did to me this morning!"

"Tell me all about it!" says Lisa.

Jill pours out her heart to Lisa. Lisa sympathizes with her feelings. When Jill calms down, Lisa helps her to see the events from Rose's point of view.

"I guess Rose is still my friend," says Jill. "Boy, I sure was mad at her when I first saw you. Thanks for listening!"

Listening to gossip is good if you do so in order to rebuke the speaker and show why gossiping is wrong. In such instances, however, your rebuke must be couched in gentle terms and without self-righteousness. It must be intended for the good of the gossiper, who may have been carried away by momentary feelings or simply unaware that gossiping is wrong. Sometimes a speaker is not aware of having engaged in gossip. Words of kindly rebuke will often prevent further harm, both to the speaker, who will not continue to spread gossip once fully informed, and to the subject, since the story will go no farther. Rebukes do not always succeed, but it is your duty to try. We are all responsible for one another!

"Dave, I'm sorry to hear you say such awful things about Jared. That doesn't sound like you, to be so angry and repeat all that gossip. Wouldn't you feel better if you just worked things out with him instead of saying all this? I'd be more comfortable right now if I were seeing the side of you that's so nice to everybody."

"Yeah, Simon, you're right. I don't know what got into me. I don't really have anything against Jared. Thanks for thinking so much of me."

There is no point in listening to gossip just for the purpose of rebuke or refutation if you know that the gossiper will not pay attention to your words. In that case just walk away, and at least you will have decreased the wrong by lending one less set of ears!

Even if the information is already known to you, it is still wrong to listen to gossip.

WHY WE GOSSIP

The attraction of gossip is very great. Many people think that they benefit from participating in gossip. They may feel that gossiping enables them to advance in their social relationships and employment. They may feel that gossip is harmless entertainment. If we think carefully about it, we will see that the benefits of gossip are illusory. At best they are temporary advantages that are more than offset by long-term losses. Let us examine the supposed benefits of gossip in order to understand why we have more to gain by refraining from it.

Many people gossip in an effort to be popular. They imagine that by cutting up others they will gain a reputation for being witty, clever, and fun to be with. They may fear that if they refrain from gossip they will appear foolish and dull-witted.

In some circles gossiping is a requirement. People who do not play along are soon excluded. Many join in for fear of being ostracized.

Some employers make gossiping a virtual requirement of employment. While claiming to use gossip to maintain employee interest, the employer's actual purpose is to divide the co-workers from one another, preventing them from developing any true commonality of interest. The employer may feel threatened by employee unity or may feel that employees isolated by an atmosphere of mistrust will work harder. Such an employer may reward those workers who are most ready to tell the secrets of their co-workers. Workers who do not play along may find themselves left out of promotions and raises, even if they perform their assigned tasks well. As a result, workers may feel that their livelihood is dependent upon their participation in gossip.

The defenders of gossip claim that it generates intimacy. By keeping the grapevine going, gossip keeps people in touch with one another. Some psychologists and social scientists have commended gossip as the glue that keeps a community together. This may be true if they mean news of births and deaths and the kinds of information we find in the legal notices in the local newspaper. It is not true if they mean revealing nasty secrets about people. News is necessary for human society, but gossip destroys society.

The argument that gossip promotes intimacy is a powerful motivation for gossip. The world is such a lonely place! We long for true connection with other human beings more than we long for money, power, or fame. Engaging in gossip makes us feel that we are deeply involved with others. If we are sharing other people's secrets and learning the most private details of their lives, then we must really be closely connected to them, right? When we mention that we have a juicy piece of gossip to share, everyone leans in close to hear. We feel that we are at the center of a real little community. For this moment, we are not so alone.

THE TRUE EFFECT OF GOSSIP

Upon reflection we will see that gossip cannot help us to achieve friendship or intimacy. If we need to gossip to keep our friends or our job, it is usually not worth it.

Gossip is the basis for some friendships. There is no guarantee that you can stop gossiping and still keep all of your old friends. If the people you socialize with do nothing but gossip, they may start to avoid you once you decide not to participate in this kind of talk. Everyone recognizes that people who do not gossip are superior to people who do gossip. Nobody likes a constant reminder that he or she is an inferior person. Some of your old friends may find themselves feeling uncomfortable in the presence of a better sort of person, a person who does not engage in gossip.

"Arlene used to be one of us, but lately she's so stuck up. She won't talk about anyone any more. Who does she think she is, some kind of angel or something? Forget about her!"

If you lose your friends because you refuse to engage in gossip, please ask yourself this: "What have I really lost?" Didn't you gossip about those very friends? Weren't you sure that whenever you were not present they were gossiping about you? You can be sure that out of your earshot they were constantly repeating your faults, real and imagined. Isn't it true that when you socialize with habitual gossipers your friendship is held together by fear more than by love? You have to keep up with the group to keep from being torn apart by them. Is this friendship?

The thought of giving up your current friends may be terrifying, but you can be sure that there are other people out there, people who do not insist on constantly criticizing others as the price of admission to their intimate circle. If giving up gossip causes you to lose your old friends, the end result will be that you will end up with true friends, friends you can depend upon when you are not with them, friends who will back you up and defend you. How do you make such friends? The first step is to be such a friend, by never gossiping about others.

The argument that gossip generates intimacy is a complete falsehood. The truth is exactly the opposite. Gossip creates walls between us and other people. Those you gossip about will hear of it and become wary of you. You will keep your distance from people you know to be gossipers. You will be afraid to share with others your deepest thoughts and feelings, for fear that they will become the material for mockery by strangers. Think about it! Don't you know from your own experience that the momentary sense of intimacy created by gossip is soon displaced by a greater feeling of loneliness? The habitual gossiper is always alone, even if surrounded by people day and night. Nobody is truly "with" him, nor he with them.

True intimacy is possible, but there is no shortcut. The way to be intimate is to be a real friend. Instead of talking about people, try listening to them. Lend a sympathetic ear to hear about their pains and their troubles. Show that you care about what is really on their minds. Find out what issues really matter to your friends, and solicit their opinions on these issues. Never speak against your friends behind their backs. They will come to trust you and value you. You will know true intimacy. The possibility of real intimacy and true friendship is one of the greatest reasons to refrain from gossip.

SOCIAL PRESSURE TO GOSSIP

You may be tempted to gossip by pressure from friends, family, co-workers, or employer. Your friends may insist that you tell them whatever "juicy tidbits" you know about mutual acquaintances, particularly if they are aware that you are privy to some secret. A parent or a teacher might pressure you to tell on others. An employer might make engaging in gossip a virtual condition of employment or a prerequisite for advancement.

"Sally, weren't you at that school board meeting where Jeff made a fool of himself trying to undermine the superintendent? Tell us all about it!"

"All right, who threw those spitballs?" the teacher demanded. "Nobody will be dismissed until I find out. Steve, you tell me! Who did it?"

"Dorothy, I hope you like working here. I think you have a lot of potential in this line of work. Look, do me a favor! If you happen to notice that any of your co-workers are coming back late from lunch or just not getting much done, how about dropping me a friendly little memo about it, OK? I think you could demonstrate that you're a real team player."

Social pressure is not an acceptable reason to engage in gossip. If your friends will not respect your desire to keep from gossiping, you might reconsider the value of passing time with people who are so disrespectful of your values. Besides, do you want to be with people who are so insensitive to the difference between right and wrong? If someone in authority, such as a teacher or an employer, pressures you to gossip, refuse respectfully and make it clear that you will not compromise your principles.

"Mrs. Cogsworth, I can tell you for sure that I wasn't the one who threw those spitballs. I'm afraid I can't say anything more about it. I am sorry that you had to suffer this disrespect."

"Ms. Thompson, I intend to work really hard around here, and I'm sure you'll see that I can do you a lot of good by backing you up in your tasks and keeping our supervisor and the customers happy. I'm afraid that I won't be able to say anything about my fellow employees, since I don't consider myself qualified to judge their contributions to the company. I do try not to talk about people, boss, and you will see how well I keep your confidence."

Refusals to engage in gossip sometimes result in personal losses. You may lose friends that you value. You may get into trouble with a person in authority. You may lose your job and the ability to support your family. This is most unfortunate, but even if you suffer a great material loss, your integrity is your greatest possession. Possessions can be lost or stolen, but nobody can take away your determination to do what is right. As long as you can live with yourself and take pride in your own actions, you will eventually recover from whatever loss you may suffer. You may never again find such promising employment. You may get a lower grade that hurts your chances for college or future employment. You may have a hard time finding new friends. Have faith that there is a relationship between means and ends. If you have to compromise yourself to achieve some goal, then that goal will not bring you the happiness you had hoped for, even if you should reach it. If you live the right way at all times, then whatever you do achieve will be a source of pride for you.

My own experience is that one never loses in the long run by refusing to engage in gossip. Whatever loss you suffer by not gossiping, you will soon see that you have lost nothing but the opportunity to make yourself miserable. In the end you will come out ahead because you will gain a reputation as a trustworthy person.

WHAT TO TALK ABOUT

There are plenty of things to talk about that are much more interesting than gossip. Always keep this rule in mind:

Talk about things that are important in the life of the person with whom you are talking.

If you make this rule your guide, you probably will never have to worry about what kinds of speech are prohibited as gossip. Your conversation will automatically take a positive turn.

Think for a moment about the things that really matter in your life and the lives of your friends:

The difficulty of raising children.

The cost of living.

The weather.

Hopes for the future.

The tasks you are fulfilling at work.

Your educational advancement.

Volunteer work and commitments.

If you talk to your friends about these things as they arise in their lives, you will not need to turn the conversation to a discussion about anyone else. If I love you, I will want to talk with you about the things that are important in your life. Unless I love you enough to care about what is on your mind, why would you want to talk with me?

Consider this saying about people and the things they talk about:

It is refined to talk about issues. It is common to talk about events. It is vulgar to talk about other people.

Of course, no one's conversation remains in only one of these categories at all times. We all gossip on occasion. But the more we keep our conversations on a high level, the more refined we will appear to be in the eyes of others.

People of the finest sort are distinguished from crude people not by their income nor by the clothes they wear, nor by their accents, but by the topics they choose to discuss. Those who speak about interesting ideas are welcomed in any worthy circle, even if they cannot compare to others in income or family tree.

There are so many issues worthy of discussion. We live in a democracy in which it is important for every citizen to be well informed. It is always good to discuss the political topics of the day, from great issues like peace between nations to local issues like trash recycling.

When the conversation turns to more immediate considerations, there are many events that are worthy of discussion. If you are a sports fan, you can discuss the standings and the performance of your favorite teams in recent games. You can tell about your recent experiences and ask your friends about theirs. Most people have personal interests and hobbies. If you prod them a little, they will be happy to talk about these things, and most people are very interesting when they talk about the things that excite them personally. And there is always the weather—ever changing, always relevant.

There are not so many avid Bible readers as once there were. In the days when nearly all people were conversant with the Bible, this great book provided an endless source of conversation on topics of interest and great relevance to human life. Discussions of sacred Scripture are elevated above all gossip, and they elevate those who engage in them to a higher level of being. The Bible still has the potential to fulfill this role for those who seek out social circles where religious study is valued. The Bible remains the greatest common source for worthy discussion topics—who are we, and what God demands of us.

My brother Eli Wylen once said, *"When you discuss David the King, this is conversation on the highest level. When you discuss David your next-door neighbor, who may be doing some of the same things, this is gossip."*

How true!

Chapter 3
Judgment

All the ways of a person seem right to him, but God probes motives.

—Proverbs 16:2

Hillel said: "Do not judge another until you have stood in his place."

—Avot 2:5

In the light of what was said in the last chapter, one might think it is sufficient to live by the rule, "Never say anything bad about anyone." It would be easy to avoid gossip if we could just say nice things about everyone all the time. Unfortunately, this easy solution to the problem of gossip is not a good one. Proper speech is but one component of a higher goal—to increase goodness in the world by improving ourselves and the society we live in. To do this we must constantly make judgments. As much as we praise what is good, just, and right, we must be prepared to condemn what is wrong, unjust, and perverse. To judge is a moral obligation. No society can exist without courts of justice in which those accused of crimes are tried and, if found guilty, convicted and punished. No community or informal society can exist without rules of conduct that are enforced by its members. Fear of public disapproval is a more powerful deterrent to crime than the threat of punishment by an impersonal legal system. This is one reason that crime rates are lowest in traditional societies and in small communities in which everyone knows one other. Every good citizen publicly praises what is good and condemns what is bad.

There exists a rather extreme form of humanism that is willing to validate every human deed just because it was committed by a human being, since "man is the measure of all things." In Judaism such complete moral relativism is not acceptable. Besides, common sense tells us that it is not reasonable to be so optimistic about human nature as to suppose that anything that any person chooses to do is good.

We do have a high regard for the human being. Every one of us has a unique aesthetic sense, a personal capacity to appreciate and enjoy the world, the ability to interact with other human beings and to make moral decisions. Every human being is of infinite value. The Bible says that every human being is created "in the image of God" (Genesis 1:27). This does not mean that every human being is perfect, a god unto himself, but rather that every human being has the capacity to choose between good and evil. It follows from this that we are held to account for the moral choices we make.

Mark Chapman, the killer of John Lennon, announced on the tenth anniversary of his crime that he is really a good person. "A person should not be judged by what he did in just one moment of his life," Chapman proclaimed. If we look at him as a whole person, Chapman said, he's a pretty wonderful guy, just like you and me.

The following is a true account:

When President Ronald Reagan announced his intention to lay a wreath at the German military cemetery in Bitburg, the famous Holocaust survivor Elie Wiesel publicly asked the President not to grant this honor to the S.S. soldiers who were buried there. While this controversy was raging, a philosophy professor asked to speak to me. "Those S.S. soldiers should be forgiven already," he said to me, "because their actions during the Holocaust were human, and since they were human they must be excused. But you Jews will not forgive and forget, and for that there is no excuse. You deserve to be condemned for this."

Such is the illogical outcome of the view that no human being may judge another—in the end, the guilty go unpunished and the innocent are condemned! The talmudic sages noticed this same illogic in the human character. They saw that the biblical King Saul was indulgent to King Agag of Amalek (the Hitler of his day), but soon afterwards tried to hunt down and kill the innocent David. The sages said, "Those who are kind to the cruel will, in the end, be cruel to the kind" (Ecclesiastes Rabba 7:16).

Jews believe that human beings are born neither good nor evil, but with a capacity for both. Christians believe in original sin. Despite their theological differences, Jews and Christians agree that no one is sinless, and that all human beings are desperately in need of grace, forgiveness, and self-improvement.

The Jewish laws of prohibited speech were composed and ordered by people who believed that at every moment they were standing before the throne of judgment. They did not resist the tremendous sense of guilt that inevitably results from studying the rules about gossip. That guilt only confirmed their conviction that we humans are a pretty sinful bunch of creatures. It seemed to them that overcoming sin was what life is all about. If we of today tend to turn aside from teachings that make us feel guilty, it may be because we do not like to be shaken in our belief in the natural perfection of the human species. Or it may be that we are less confident than our ancestors in the existence of a loving, forgiving God who will ultimately relieve us of our burden of guilt.

HOW TO JUDGE

How can we stand in judgment over a creature so awesome, so worthy of dignity and respect, as another human being? The basic rule for judging others is this: *People are judged by their deeds*.

Several people were talking about Carl, who had just been sent to jail after being in and out of trouble with the law for many years. "He's not a bad person," said Leonard, "he's just done some bad things."

Leonard has missed the point. No one is a bad person by nature. A "bad person" is someone who does bad things. There is no other acceptable definition.

We cannot judge the inner thoughts of others, nor the state of their souls. All we truly know about other people is what they do before the eyes of the world. It is not hypocritical or overly bold to make judgments about others on the basis of what our five senses reveal to us. We must only make certain that our judgments are proper, according to the rules that we shall discuss below.

JUDGING OTHERS

The most important thing to remember when judging the deeds of another person is this: *Judge others to be righteous.*

The original Hebrew adage tells us to place all others in the "cup of acquittal" on the balance scale of justice. This is not the same as suspending all judgment and excusing all wrongs. It means that we must attribute the best possible motives and intentions to other people's actions, even when those actions are improper. All the more so are we obligated to presume that the permissible actions of others are motivated by sincere and good intentions. We should not look for ulterior motives in the good deeds of other people.

"Of course Ed always picks up the check," said Frank. "He likes to appear like a big shot."

Does anyone know why Ed always picks up the check? Judging others to be righteous—attributing the best possible motive—Frank should say,

"Ed is a generous person. He likes to do for others. He always picks up the check when we go out."

Another example:

Alicia says to Laura, "Karen is always so sweet to her husband." Laura replies, "Why shouldn't she be? He buys her everything she wants. She has him wrapped around her little finger."

It is ungenerous of Laura to presume that Karen is nice to her husband only because he buys her things. For all Laura knows, Karen would be just as nice to him if he were a pauper or a miser. Laura should presume that Karen is sweet to her husband because she really loves him and because she has a kind and gentle disposition.

Matt said to Jared, "You should have seen the Browns at the party last Saturday. They were kissing up to the Everlys all night, but they hardly had a word for the Elkinds. Those Browns only make friends with rich people who can help them climb the social ladder."

It may be completely true that the Browns sought out the Everlys at the party and ignored the Elkinds. Matt saw this with his own eyes. But it does not follow that the Browns are social climbers, just because the Everlys are wealthy and the Elkinds are not. It may be that the Browns crave the friendship of the Everlys because they find them interesting and admirable. The Browns just may not feel comfortable with the Elkinds. The Browns might still seek out the Everlys and avoid the Elkinds even if their social standing were reversed.

Only God knows our true motives. The Nobel Prize–winning author I. B. Singer said that it ruins a story for an author to provide a clear motive for the actions of his characters. Fiction, said Singer, should imitate real life, in which motivation is always beyond comprehension. Most of us do not even know our own reasons for doing what we do. How can we hope, then, to know what motivates the actions of others? The only safe course is to assume the best, to judge others to be righteous.

If someone insults you, assume that it was inadvertent, and that the perpetrator of the insult would feel terrible to know that you had been hurt.

If someone takes more than a fair share, assume that it was not clear what a proper share was, for otherwise he or she would have taken only what was appropriate, minus a little for generosity's sake.

If you see someone doing wrong, assume that he or she did not know that the act was wrong. It must have seemed that the deed was permitted in this particular case. The person is in need of education.

If someone is late in repaying a debt, assume that he or she is short of money at the moment but will repay you as soon as possible. If in the meantime you see the same person purchase something else, assume that she did so with money that was not available for any other purpose, or that it was a necessary expense.

The following story is told in the Talmud (Shabbat 127b):

A workman came to his employer, a wealthy landowner, to collect his wages so that he could go home for the New Year holiday. The workman said to his employer, "Give me my wages."

The landowner said, "I'm sorry, I have no money."

"Very well," said the workman. "Pay me with a share of your crops!"

"I have no crops," said the landowner.

"Then," said the workman, "pay me with land!"

"I have no land," said the employer.

"All right," said the workman. "Pay me with animals."

"I have no animals," said the employer.

"Well, then," said the workman, "I will accept household goods as my salary."

"I have no household goods," said the wealthy employer.

The workman was disappointed but said nothing. He left for home without any provisions for the holiday.

After the holiday the employer came to the workman's door with the man's wages in his hand and leading three donkeys laden with food, drink, and delicacies. The employer handed his workman his wages in cash and presented the loaded donkeys as a gift.

"What did you think of me," asked the employer, "when I told you I had no money to give you?"

The workman replied, "I thought that all of your money was tied up in an investment."

"And what did you think when I told you I had no crops?"

"I thought that you had not yet tithed your crops and so you considered them to be God's and not your own."

"And when I said I had no land?"

"I presumed you had rented your land to another."

"And what did you think when I said I had no animals?"

"I presumed that you had let out all of your animals for hire," said the workman.

"And when I said I had no household goods?"

"I presumed that you had vowed all of your possessions to God."

The employer said, "It is all just as you said! Because you judged me to be righteous and did not accuse me, I have brought you these gifts, and may God judge you as favorably as you have judged me!"

The Jewish philosopher Hermann Cohen taught that in the highest sense no sins are intentional. Every sin results from lack of knowledge or from mistaken judgment. No one would ever harm another person if we were truly wise enough to foresee the outcome of our actions.

If you judge everyone to be righteous, you will acquire deep insight into human nature. Most people justify to themselves whatever they do. As it is said, "everyone is righteous in his own eyes." If you judge the deeds of others by the best possible motive, you will understand them as they understand themselves. We may think we are being profound when we "expose" the selfish and evil motives of others, but the truth is just the opposite. The more we judge others to be righteous, the closer we come to truly understanding them.

AMBIGUOUS STATEMENTS

Most human deeds are neither purely good nor purely bad. They contain a mixture of good and bad, and much depends upon point of view. Most of what we say about others is neither pure praise nor pure criticism. Much of what we say is ambiguous. It could be taken either way, depending on the perspective that we or our listeners take toward the deeds that we are describing.

Whether your statement about someone else is understood as praise or criticism depends upon many factors. To name a few:

The circumstances surrounding the events you are describing.

The circumstances in which you retell the story.

The character of the person about whom you speak.

The character of the people with whom you are speaking.

The feelings of your listeners toward the subject.

Your attitude, posture, and tone of voice.

In most cases we need to use good judgment to decide whether an ambiguous statement about another person is permissible news or forbidden gossip.

If you are at your cooking club and you say, "Oscar made a great chocolate cake this week," this is clearly intended as praise. If you say the same thing at a Weight Watchers meeting, it is gossip.

If John is poor and you say to your friends, "I happen to know that John gave a hundred dollars to the United Way this year," that is praise (even though you probably shouldn't be repeating this privileged information). If John is wealthy, then repeating the same information may be gossip. It depends, as well, on how your listeners feel about United Way, and how they feel about John.

If you say in front of a group of Ethel's best friends, "Ethel is the front-runner to be made the next partner in the firm," it is praise. If you say the same thing in front of Ethel's enemies, they will understand that you are giving them an opening to discuss how unworthy she is of this honor. They will take your statement as implied criticism of Ethel as an office climber and a backstabber.

If you say in a positive, excited tone of voice, "Mark finally made a basket after twenty misses," everyone will understand that you are sharing Mark's excitement at finally learning how to play basketball. You are praising him for his efforts to improve. If you say the same thing in a droll voice and with raised eyebrows, your statement is gossip. We will then understand that you are pointing out how Mark is still a pathetic athlete, despite his great efforts.

Before saying anything about another person, consider not only the content of your statement, but also how it will be interpreted. Regardless of your intentions, your statement will actually mean what people think it means. If you are speaking about someone whom your audience dislikes, they will try to find the bad in everything you say. Thus extra caution is required to make it clear that you intend only to elevate your subject in the esteem of his enemies. If you are speaking about a person you are known to dislike, your audience will assume that you intend to criticize, and even statements of clear praise will be taken as irony. It is safest to avoid ambiguous statements about those who are not well liked and to avoid altogether discussing the deeds or character of your own enemies. It is not right to say, "Well, I didn't really say anything bad, and if people take it that way, that's their problem." This attitude is an opening for backhanded gossip. We are all responsible for the statements that flow from our own lips. They are the children that we have sent out into the world, and we have to tend them.

EVALUATIVE AND JUDGMENTAL LANGUAGE

Very often it is necessary, in the course of conversation, to mention someone else's deeds. When you do this, choose your words carefully. Your language should be purely *descriptive*, never *evaluative* or *judgmental*. It is best to avoid evaluative language altogether, even if your evaluation is positive. We are always on safe ground if we describe what we have seen or experienced in entirely neutral terms. For example:

Negative Evaluation: Bob is a drunkard.

Positive Evaluation: Bob is a real party guy.

Neutral Description: Bob usually has three or more drinks at a party.

Negative Evaluation: Sharon is a compulsive shopper. She buys lots of clothes she doesn't even need.

Positive Evaluation: Sharon is a really fashionable person. She is always wearing the latest thing.

Neutral Description: Sharon owns many clothes.

Negative Evaluation: Richard is a real huckster.

Positive Evaluation: Richard is an innovative entrepreneur.

Neutral Description: Richard is often involved in new businesses.

Negative Evaluation: Tucker overeats.

Positive Evaluation: Tucker is a gourmet.

Neutral Description: Tucker eats a great deal.

There is no right or wrong in matters of taste. It is not for us to decide what is best for others as long as they remain within the confines of what is legal and moral. If we train ourselves to avoid evaluative and judgmental language, we will learn to be objective about others. At the least, we will learn to distinguish between our own opinions and the rights of others to act as they wish within the bounds of decency. We will be less likely to gossip about others when we are careful to distinguish the facts from our opinion of the facts. This is why it is good to avoid even positive judgments about others. It helps us to build good habits in the way we think about other people.

Often we leap to conclusions and then present them as facts. It takes lots of effort to sort out and separate our opinions from our observations.

"I saw Gloria taking advantage of poor Grandpa."

"You did? Tell me what you actually saw."

"She kept asking him for money until she had him so befuddled that he gave it to her."

"What you saw, then, was Gloria repeatedly requesting money, and Grandpa giving it to her. How do you know she was taking advantage of him? Maybe he encourages her to play up to him before he gives her what she wants because he enjoys the interaction?"

"Well, that may be, but it seemed to me that she was taking advantage of him."

"Ah, so this is your opinion. The only thing we can say for sure is that Grandpa gave Gloria money."

"Yeah. I sure wish he would give me some money!"

"Maybe you're just envious of Gloria's close relationship to Grandpa and the way he gives her things."

"Well, that could be. Let me think about it."

CHARACTER TRAITS

We should not mention anyone's faulty character traits. It is equally wrong to say that a person *lacks* any positive character trait, even if that trait is rarely found.

The following statements are all improper:

"I saw Leon playing basketball the other day. Boy, for an athlete, he sure is a klutz!"

"I saw Leon playing basketball the other day. He does not have the grace and quickness that one usually sees in basketball players."

"I saw Leon playing basketball the other day. When it comes to moves, he's no Michael Jordan!"

The first of the three statements mentions a negative character trait, klutziness. The second statement mentions the lack of a positive trait, grace and quickness. The third statement only affirms that Leon lacks a quality which is lacking in many basketball players, including most professionals in the N.B.A.—namely, the skills of a Michael Jordan. Even so, it has the same effect as the first two statements, which is to lower Leon in the esteem of those who admire basketball talent.

Please recall that gossip is any statement which lowers a person in the esteem of others. Even a lowering from infinite esteem to merely great esteem is still a decrease. This is the danger in suggesting that there are limits to someone's positive character traits.

Amy and Brett are discussing the teachers in their various college classes. Brett says to Amy, "Our physics professor, Mr. Jones, is smarter than any physicist of the modern era, except maybe Einstein." Amy is surprised to hear this. She has always regarded Mr. Jones as smarter than Einstein. She felt privileged to be studying with the most brilliant physicist of all time. Of course, she doesn't mention this to Brett. She doesn't want to seem a gullible fool. But in her mind Amy says, "I guess Mr. Jones isn't really as smart as I thought he was."

Brett intended only to praise Mr. Jones, his teacher. Even so, he gossiped against him by suggesting that he lacked a particular rare and wonderful trait—the genius of Einstein.

We must beware of exaggerating anyone's fine traits in front of others, especially his or her enemies. The listeners may be tempted to give a more balanced estimate of your subject by mentioning some faults. It is best to praise people lightly, so that others will say in their hearts, "Yes, she is all of that, and much more as well." In the long run we acquire or lose the respect of others by our deeds. Words of praise will not make that much difference. We should praise others just enough so that our listeners will remember and consider their good deeds.

When Rabbi Akavia ben Mehalalel was on his deathbed, his son said to him, "Father, commend me to your companions!"

Akavia said to his son, "I will not commend you."

"Have you perhaps found some fault with me?" asked the son.

"No," said his father, "but your deeds will recommend you" (Eduyot 5:7).

The following is an example of why we should not praise others too much:

After the United Way dinner, Arlene said to her companions, "The new campaign director, Mr. Apple, must be the most generous person who ever lived!"

"Oh, I don't know about that," said one of Arlene's companions. "I'd say that the outgoing director is really the more generous of the two."

Meanwhile, at another table, Shannon said to her companions, "I admire Mr. Apple for his generosity."

"Yes," said another at the table, "He is pretty giving, isn't he? They made a good choice for campaign director."

PAST WRONGS

It is gossip to mention the past misdeeds of others, whether behind their backs or to their faces.

If someone has done wrong in the past, it is generous to assume that by now he or she has made amends. Even if we know that this is not the case, we should assume that the person in question now regrets the wrong he has committed.

We should mention past wrongs only if there is some current practical benefit to be gained. If there is nothing to be gained in the present, why bring up past unpleasantness?

Sometimes people do something wrong because they are overwhelmed by a sudden and unusual temptation. If someone commits a wrong that is unlikely to be repeated, there is no point in bringing it up. Even if your intention is only righteous rebuke, your words serve no purpose. They can only bring needless shame and embarrassment to the perpetrator. Since there is no benefit to anyone from your words, it is better to remain silent.

Sarah is known in the community of writers for the excellent research work she does for the articles she writes. Once, crushed by some extraordinary family demands and pressed by a deadline for a very important article, Sarah copied large portions of another article without giving proper attribution. John, a fellow writer, finds out about this just by chance, because he recently did some work that brought him to the obscure article from which Sarah copied. John knows Sarah well. He knows the quality of her work, and since he knows the unusual circumstances facing Sarah, he can guess why she took a desperate measure. When John mentioned the title of her recent article to Sarah, she blushed and changed the subject. John can see that she wants to put this episode behind her. Since Sarah has repented her past sin and no one stands to be harmed further by it, John decides to keep silent and tell no one, even Sarah, that he knows what she did.

Sometimes a person who used to regularly do wrong has completely changed and adopted new ways. In religious tradition, such a person is called a penitent. Someone who has undergone a transformation of this kind stands before God as a new person, with the wrongs of the past forgiven. To remind the penitent of the past is like trying to stand on a higher pedestal than God. It might seem unfair to you that penitents escape the consequences of their past actions. Those who are true penitents will suffer adequately from their own regrets. We need not add to their sense of shame and guilt. One of the great incentives to repentance is the fact that we can remove ourselves from the stigma of our past misdeeds. Those who insist on constantly bringing up the former wrongs of others are committing a great wrong in that they are discouraging others from repenting. Why should they repent if they can never escape judgment for their past deeds?

Mrs. Allen could not stand to see Rabbi Levi standing in the pulpit preaching about goodness every week. "Do you know what he used to be like before he became a rabbi?" she said to everyone. "He was the worst con man in town. I'd like to have a place in heaven for every innocent person he cheated out of their honest money." When Rabbi Levi became aware that thanks to Mrs. Allen everyone now knew about his sorry misdeeds of the past, he offered his resignation. The trustees of the congregation refused to accept it. "We feel that you are a better leader," they said to him, "because you know of what you speak." Rabbi Levi thanked the trustees for their confidence, but he resigned nevertheless. He could not bear the shame of having his whole congregation know the details of his past. The synagogue lost one of the finest leaders it had ever had. Rabbi Levi went to a new town where no one knew his past. There he distinguished himself in service.

Sometimes penitents like to publicize their former misdeeds in order to keep others from making the same mistakes. Some of the world's great literature consists of the published confessions of penitents. A sports star who has ruined his career with drugs and alcohol may choose to speak in schools to warn his young fans of the dangers that lie ahead for anyone who imitates his former path. It is certainly praiseworthy for penitents to speak of their former sins when their purpose is to help others. But we should not think that we stand on the same sanctified ground when we speak of the sins of others. We are taught: The penitent stands where the saint cannot stand. He may mention his own sins, but we may not mention them to him or to others.

THREE KINDS OF PEOPLE

There are three kinds of people—the saintly, the ordinary, and the brazen wrongdoer. A saintly person is someone whose personal standards of goodness are far above the human norm. The saintly person generally acts selflessly and tries to meet the highest standards of human behavior. When we see a saintly person appearing to do wrong, we should not mention it. We should assume either that we are mistaken in our judgment of what we have seen or that the saintly person has already repented.

When we see an ordinary person doing wrong, we may mention it if our intention is only to correct his or her ways. Our words should be gentle and our intention must be loving. We should be concerned not only for what is right and good, but also for the best interests of the person we are rebuking. Ordinary people often do not realize that they are doing wrong or do not perceive the true consequences of their actions. If the rebuke is private, gentle, and full of love and concern, the person to whom it is directed may be grateful for having been set on a better course.

The habitual sinner is one who consistently does wrong, without concern for the consequences. The habitual sinner will not listen to rebuke, so there is no sense in trying. Jewish tradition teaches that it is a good deed to publicly criticize the brazen wrongdoer at every opportunity. Such a person should be made into a negative example so that other people will see that public contempt is the reward of evil.

I personally doubt whether it is a good thing to avail ourselves of the traditional permission to heap scorn on the habitual sinner. Gossip does at least as much damage to the character of the speaker as it does to the reputation of the subject. Taking advantage of this permission could make one into a habitual gossip with a bitter attitude to life. We would not want to find ourselves tainted by hatred and anger.

In the past, society operated by clear rules. Everyone knew who lived by the rules and who did not. In our times, it is hard to know what conduct would brand a person as a habitual sinner. American society is so open and our norms so unclear! Left to ourselves, we may be tempted to define as a terrible sinner anyone who has encroached upon our own imagined rights or offended our personal standards of taste. We could end up using this limited permission as a license to gossip against whomever has angered us.

It may be best, when some infamous name is brought up, merely to sigh as an indication of your sorrow that some people do not experience the joy of being good.

Fred says to Alan that he saw Bob the other day, once again drunk and out with another woman. "That Bob is a disgrace to humanity," Fred says. "Think of his poor wife and children! It's too bad they don't whip people anymore!

Alan, who is careful not to gossip, sadly shakes his head. "It is good to live a sober and responsible life," he says.

Chapter 4
Telling

God said to the tongue: "All the other parts of the body I made standing up, but I made you lying down, and I have built two walls around you."

—Arakhin 15

TALEBEARING

Talebearing is telling one person the disparaging statements made about him or her by another person. In Jewish tradition talebearing is called *rekhilut*—literally, "merchandising." As the merchant goes from place to place, buying and selling, so the talebearer goes from person to person, picking up gossip here and repeating it there.

Sheila says to Darlene, "At the auxiliary meeting last week, Amanda told everyone that you are always yelling at your husband."

Eric says to Neal, "I hate for you to think that Robbie is a good friend of yours. He's been telling everyone about the lousy car you sold him, and saying that you purposely cheated him."

Tricia says to Michael, "You should have been at the board meeting yesterday. The boss told everyone that you were the main reason our profits are down."

You may feel that a person who is the subject of gossip deserves to know about it. While your intention may be good, the result of reporting gossip to its subject will not be good. Whatever damage was done by the gossip, the hurt can only be compounded by telling the victim what has been said about him or her.

Most of the time the motive for talebearing is not noble. The talebearer may make a show of deep concern for the victim of gossip but is often is motivated by dislike for the gossiper or for the victim. Sometimes the talebearer is someone with a certain amount of innate malice, someone who enjoys seeing the sparks fly when people are angry with one another. The talebearer may find this amusing.

"Jody, I always told you that Thea was up to no good. I never liked her or trusted her. Now you should hear what terrible rumors she's spreading about you all over town."

"Ben, you poor dear! It seems like nobody likes you at all! I was at a party last night—I guess you weren't invited—and everyone there had bad things to say about you. It must be hard to be so unpopular, isn't it?"

"Diane, you really ought to have a word with Dorothy! She's telling everyone about how you made a fool of yourself when you got drunk at the office party. Believe me, I only want the best for both of you, but someone should stop her mouth, and it ought to be you!"

Sometimes the talebearer's malice is fairly obvious. In many real-life situations, however, the talebearer's true motives are carefully disguised. Beware of the intentions of anyone who claims to be doing you good by telling you how others are gossiping about you! It is better to avoid the company of such people altogether.

I can never forget one time when I was deeply hurt by talebearing. That year I was the youth group advisor in a large congregation. At the annual meeting of the congregation, one of the officers disparaged my work. I would never have known how my name was slandered before hundreds of people but for one member of my youth group who was present at the meeting. In his innocence he was so outraged for my sake that he repeated to me what had been said.

He told me this out of pure devotion to his leader, but his every word caused me great pain. I realized then that if even the most well-intentioned talebearing is hurtful and unnecessary, how much the more so when it is done with even a hint of an impure motive! I resolved to remember this incident as a warning to myself never to be a talebearer.

Some people are curious to know what others are saying about them. They may beg you or even pressure you to tell. Do not imagine that you are doing anyone a favor when you report gossip in such instances. Even when the subject of gossip gives permission to repeat it, you are not relieved of the moral imperative to refrain from talebearing. The very person who pressured you to tell will not be pleased by the gossip once you repeat it, and you could also get in trouble with the people whose private conversation you have revealed. Stay out of trouble by pleading ignorance of what has been said or, better yet, by establishing a solid reputation as a person who does not repeat gossip.

"Please tell me what others think of me."

"Tell me what Jane said about me after I broke up with her."

"I want you to let me know what the other employees say about me behind my back."

Requests of this kind should be resisted. It will be much easier for you to resist the pressure to repeat gossip if you have established a general reputation as someone who does not engage in gossip. If you do not have such a reputation, your refusal to respond to a request like those above might create suspicion that you know things too unpleasant to repeat. Try to dispel such notions by saying something like this:

"I can only speak for myself. Would you like my honest evaluation of your good points and weaknesses?"

"Whether Jane has said good things about you or bad, I do not think that it is my business to repeat them. Please ask her yourself what she thinks of you."

"Boss, I try not to participate in office gossip. I really would not be able to tell you what other people are saying about you."

WARNINGS

There are times when it becomes necessary to relate derogatory information about one person in order to save another person from harm or from material loss. It may also be necessary to transmit such information to enable someone to recover from a loss of which he is unaware. In such a case we return to the very heart of the ethical dilemma of proper speech—that while we wish to avoid gossip, sometimes it is necessary to speak disapprovingly of others. The general rule is: One may transmit derogatory information about another person in order to save your listener from harm or material loss.

It is difficult to determine when repeating uncomplimentary information about another person is necessary, and when we are simply finding an excuse to indulge our desire to gossip. The wise know that their own base impulses can mislead them into thinking that they ought to speak out against others when there is really no need. We have seen above that none of us knows the true motives for our actions. How can we know whether it is love and concern for the listener or anger and hatred for the subject that moves us to speak out? In order to distinguish necessary from unnecessary warning, Jewish tradition establishes objective criteria.

The Criteria for a Warning

1. *Relevance.* You are certain that the information you are about to relate is directly related to protecting a specific individual

from a specific harm. It is not proper to transmit a warning to the general public about someone who you think might harm or cheat others.

Jack asks you whether Ed is a good fishing partner. You know that Ed is a nice fellow and a good fisherman, but he cheats at cards. This information is not relevant and should not be brought up unless you know that Jack will play cards with Ed on the fishing trip.

2. *Factuality*. You are absolutely certain that the information which you are going to relate is completely true. You must have first-hand knowledge of the facts. For giving a warning, it is not right to repeat second-hand rumors. If you merely think that one person may plan to cheat another, this is not sufficient cause to give a warning. On the other hand, if there is a possibility of bodily harm to another person you must use your judgment concerning the seriousness of the possible offense and the likelihood of its being carried out.

Elaine has heard rumors that a certain butcher shop grinds extra fat into its hamburger. She herself has never used that butcher shop. Her friend Deborah asks her if she should buy meat from there. Since Elaine has no first-hand knowledge of the alleged wrong, she does not repeat the gossip about adding fat to the hamburger. She simply replies, "I have never used that butcher shop, so I cannot recommend it or disrecommend it."

Brett hears a rumor that Ricky intends to beat up Michael. Knowing that Ricky has a past history of violence, Brett warns Michael to beware of him. Brett is careful to present his warning as a matter of possibility, not certainty.

3. *Maintain doubt*. Even if you must give a warning about someone, you should remain in doubt as to the actual guilt or bad intentions of that person. You are warning against possible

harm. The future is never certain, and it is quite possible that the feared harm will never arise in actuality.

4. *First, rebuke!* If at all possible, it is better to persuade the offending party to undo the wrong or retract the offense than to warn the potential victim. It is not obligatory to present a rebuke if you know that your words will not be accepted, or if it is not possible, or if by giving a rebuke you would place yourself in harm's way.

Shelley tells Lauren that she intends to get even with Toby for stealing her boyfriend. Rather than warn Toby, Shelley talks Laura into changing her intentions. Laura succeeds in convincing Shelley that the best path is just to leave Toby alone. Lauren never tells Toby anything about this conversation, and no one is the worse for it.

When Brett hears that Ricky intends to beat up Michael, he thinks about confronting Ricky and trying to talk him out of it. But when he thinks of how violent and unreasonable Ricky can be, he decides it would be wiser not to rebuke him.

5. *Do not exaggerate.* You must be accurate in everything you say in your warning. Do not exaggerate the wrong. Stick to what you know for a fact. Be certain to include in your warning any mitigating factors known to you that might make the wrong seem less bad.

Justin says to Matthew, "Look, Matthew, don't get too mixed up with Alice. I have very good reason to believe that she's still deeply involved with her old boyfriend."

Justin is exaggerating the possibility of Alice hurting Matthew. It would be better for Justin to say the following:

"Matthew, I think I should tell you that I saw Alice out with her former boyfriend last night. They were only talking, not holding hands or anything, and it could have something to do with the fact that he still has a lot of Alice's stuff that she has to get back from

him. You might want to look into this, but don't jump to any conclusions. I think Alice may like you a lot."

6. *Beneficial intent.* Your only intention in giving the warning is to benefit the person who is being warned. You must be sure not to take pleasure in exposing someone you dislike.

Arthur considers warning Ron not to enter into a business partnership with Alan. He feels they would not get along and the business would fail, with possible financial loss to Ron. Upon further consideration, Arthur realizes that his judgment is definitely clouded by his intense dislike for Alan. He realizes that he does not want his friend Ron to be involved with his enemy. Realizing that at least part of his intention is to hurt Alan, Arthur decides not to give Ron his business advice in this matter.

7. *No recourse.* There is no other way to stop the wrong. You have no recourse except to speak against the transgressor.

8. *The punishment fits the crime.* You must be absolutely certain that the wronged party will not respond in a manner that is disproportionate to the wrong. Do not be a party to private vengeance or vigilante justice!

Eli finds out that Max is being swindled. Eli knows that Max is a violent person. Max has been implicated in certain murders, though never convicted. Eli knows that if the swindlers were turned in to the police they would probably receive a short jail sentence at most. Considering the possibility that the swindlers would be murdered if Max knew how they had taken him, Eli decides not to tell Max anything.

9. *The victim is innocent in matters of this nature.* You are only obligated to give warning if the potential victim would consider the deed wrong if he or she were the perpetrator.

Elaine accidentally finds out who broke into the warehouse owned by a local fence and stole a large quantity of "hot" goods. Since the fence is himself a thief, Elaine is under no obligation to protect him from other thieves. She does not speak up.

"Honest Bob" Jones is a car dealer who is known to make used cars look better than they are and sell them for exorbitant prices. Gil finds out that some of Honest Bob's dissatisfied customers plan to torch his store. While Bob is guilty of taking advantage of gullible customers, he has certainly never done anything that is the moral equivalent to burning down a business. Gil tells Honest Bob of the plan so that he can take proper steps to protect himself.

If you know something that will protect another person from harm or prevent a material loss, it is your duty to transmit the necessary information whether or not it is requested, provided that the above conditions are met. Your obligation to give warning is even greater if you are specifically asked for the pertinent information.

LISTENING TO A WARNING

It is permissible to listen to derogatory information about someone if you need that information in order to protect yourself from harm or to recover a loss.

If the information involves a possible future loss, then you are not permitted to believe it. However, you may take steps to protect yourself in case the information should prove to be true.

Kari hears that Sue is so angry with her that she intends to come over and pull all of her hair out. Kari does not believe that Sue would do this. But just to be on the safe side, she avoids Sue for a while.

Jeff hears that Joe takes unfair advantage of his business partners. Joe comes to Jeff with a business proposition. Jeff does not believe what he has heard about Joe, but to protect himself from possible loss he declines to go into business with Joe. The proposition sounds so good, however, that Jeff decides to accept, but he plans to watch

Joe a little more closely than he normally would. This caution is permissible, as long as Jeff does not take it for a fact that Joe cheats his partners.

Marna hears rumors that Bruce is abusive toward his dates. She does not accept the rumors as facts, but when Bruce asks her out she declines, to protect herself from possible harm.

If someone attempts to warn you about another person, you should immediately interrupt and ask whether you need to know this information for some specific reason. If the reply is affirmative, then you may listen, but first you must resolve that you will not believe what you hear, but only use it to protect yourself. If the answer to your question is no, then you should respond, "Thank you for your concern, but I do not care to listen to gossip."

INQUIRING ABOUT ANOTHER PERSON TO PROTECT YOURSELF

If you are about to enter into a business or personal relationship with someone, you may need to know certain things in order to protect yourself against possible harm or loss. In such instances it is acceptable to obtain the pertinent information by inquiring of others.

Restrict your inquiry to what is necessary and relevant. Resolve not to believe what you hear but only to use it as a caution.

Boris asks Eugene for a personal loan. Before lending him the money, Eugene asks around to see if Boris is creditworthy.

Charlotte wants to back a new shop, and she wants to offer Ailene half the business to be the managing partner. Charlotte asks around to find out if Ailene is hardworking and capable. One of the people she asks wants to talk about Ailene's personal life, but Charlotte refuses to listen, since it is not relevant to her business relationship with Ailene.

Ruth is considering asking Cheryl to go with her on an auto trip across the country. Ruth first makes inquiry to find out if Cheryl is easygoing and a pleasant conversationalist.

Before taking Mike as a roommate, Peter asks around to find out if he is neat and clean and if he pays his bills promptly.

When seeking necessary information, do not inquire of a person's enemies or competitors, but only of people who will be objective. Make it clear why you are inquiring so that they will know you are not interested in gossip for its own sake. Decline to listen to any proffered information that is not relevant to your inquiry.

SPEAKING UP TO PROTECT YOURSELF FROM HARM OR LOSS

You may speak against someone in order to recover a loss or to protect yourself from harm. Do not speak against your oppressor to everyone, but only to those who can help you to recover your loss or protect yourself. If there is no hope of recovery, then you should not speak against the person who harmed you just for the sake of revenge.

If one of your friends takes your bat and ball and insists that they belong to him, you may speak to his parents to get your property back. Your friend will obey his parents, and they will know if the bat and ball are not his. There is no reason to tell all the other kids who took your bat and ball, since that will not help you get them back.

REFERENCES

You are under a moral obligation to speak the truth about others, even if you must repeat derogatory information, if withholding the truth could lead to bodily harm or material loss to the one who inquires of you.

In any other case in which you are asked to give a reference, you do not have to say anything, but if you do speak, you owe it to yourself to be completely honest. You must protect your own reputation for integrity and insight. If you speak only the truth, your good referrals for worthy individuals will be treated with the respect they deserve.

If someone asks you to be a reference, you may accept or decline. If you do not think you can give a good reference, you should try to gently decline the honor.

References are often no longer private. You invite trouble, possibly even a lawsuit, by giving a bad reference in writing. If there is a waiver to sign, making a reference form completely private, you may wish to insist that it be signed. If it is not signed, the reference is not as valuable, a point you can use to gain privacy without implying that you intend to say anything negative.

There is always something nice that you can say about any one. An honest referral that says only nice things can still be sufficient to deny someone a position for which you do not think he or she is qualified. You need only refrain from crediting the person with the specific qualities that potential employers are most interested in.

WHEN A CRIME HAS BEEN OR WILL BE COMMITTED

If you have information concerning a crime, you must report it to the proper authorities. This is an absolute moral and civic obligation and is not to be considered gossip or talebearing.

In some situations your obligation to report a crime is greater than your obligation to maintain a confidence. You must alert the proper authorities if you know for a fact that someone plans to do bodily harm to himself or to others. You must alert the proper authorities if you have information concerning the physical or sexual abuse of a child.

WHEN YOU SHOULD NOT REPORT A CRIME

In the United States of America, the rule of law is firmly established. All people receive equal treatment before the law. There was a time when members of many minority groups could not be assured of a fair trial in America, but we are fast putting those times behind us. One can be reasonably certain that anyone arrested for a crime in this country will receive a fair trial and a fair sentence. It is therefore your moral obligation to report all crimes.

Duly constituted courts of law are considered to be God's representative on earth for the purpose of administering justice. Punishments meted out by a court are not vengeance but justice. It is necessary to bring criminals to justice for the safety of others and the protection of society.

This does not apply in a country where the arbitrary decrees of the rulers are above the law or in situations where the punishment administered by the government is likely to be excessive and unjust.

At one time Jewish law held that no Jew should inform to the government against another Jew. This law came into practice in times and places where Jews could not receive fair trials because they were not treated as equal citizens. Any punishment meted out to a Jew by an anti-Semitic totalitarian ruler was likely to be unduly harsh. Moreover, even if the Jewish defendant was really guilty, it was likely that the government would not stop at punishing him but would exact a terrible retribution against the entire Jewish community, sweeping away the innocent with the guilty. In many parts of the world today it may still be necessary for oppressed minorities to defend themselves by not reporting a crime committed by one of their members.

You should not inform against a person when his trial will be politically motivated and not based on principles of justice. In a totalitarian country that does not allow emigration, for instance, this would apply to informing against an endangered person who is trying to escape.

TELLING ON CHILDREN FOR THEIR OWN GOOD

In general we do not want to report the bad deeds of others except when necessary to protect the innocent. It is a different matter with children, however, for in a sense children are innocent victims of their own bad deeds. They do not yet know any better. They need to be instructed. Even if children know they are doing something wrong, they may not realize the full consequences of their deeds. It is therefore a moral obligation to tell on children to their parents or teachers, or whoever has authority over them. Your intention must be for the guidance and improvement of the child, and not to take vengeance or show up the parents.

Sheila calls all the mothers of the other six-year-olds in the neighborhood. "You'd better get some control over your little boy!" she says. "My Mortimer tells me that your son and the other boys were breaking windows today, and they forced him to join them. My Mortimer would never do such things if it were not for the bad influence of children like yours."

Sheila should not be speaking this way, because her intention is not right. If her intention were to discipline her son and all the other children to teach them that it is wrong to destroy property, then she would be doing good in calling the other mothers and fathers.

MAKING AN EXAMPLE OF SOMEONE

You may on occasion point out a totally disreputable person as an example to your children or to others who would genuinely benefit from such instruction. Before making an example of someone, one should consider these five conditions:

1. You know as an absolute fact that the person has committed an offense. It is not just a matter of rumor.
2. The deeds committed by the person are truly evil.
3. You do not exaggerate.
4. Your intention is only the moral improvement of your listeners. It is not to take malicious pleasure in reciting the misdeeds of another. You are not motivated by personal dislike for the wrongdoer.
5. You are not two-faced with the wrongdoer. You do not pretend to like him or approve of him to his face, except out of fear of retribution.

Well, children, Mr. Green from down the street was convicted today of dealing drugs. They gave him twenty-five years in prison. I know you were impressed with his fancy clothes and his expensive cars. I hope you learn from what happened to Mr. Green that in the long run crime does not pay. Selling drugs is not a quick way to success. Now, go do your homework!

Just as you may make an example of a blatant evildoer for the instruction of your household, you may also prohibit the members of your household or those under your guidance from interacting with those of whose actions you disapprove.

"Children, I do not want to see you with Jennifer Brown who lives on Second Avenue, and I do not want you to talk with her. Her repeated absences from school and her arrests for shoplifting make her a bad influence in my eyes. I hope that you sympathize with her for all her troubles, but I know that she has professional counselors

who are trying to get her straightened out. For your own sake it would be best for you not to get too involved with her."

"Honey, I would prefer that you do not spend too much time with your new co-worker, Lolita. She is on her fourth marriage, and three of those husbands were married when she met them. I would be unhappy if you were to become her fifth husband. I am not saying that you or she would do anything to hurt me, but I feel it would avoid problems for you to remain very professional in your dealings with her."

Chapter 5
Prevarication, Prejudice, Public Figures, Promises, Profanity: A Potpourri

The seal of the Blessed Holy One is truth.
—Shabbat 55

Train yourself to say "I do not know," lest you accidentally make yourself a liar.
—Berakhot 4

Having decided to create humankind, the Blessed Holy One consulted the angels. The angel of justice said, "Create humankind, because they will strive to be just." The angel of truth said, "Do not create humankind, for they shall not be truthful." What did the Blessed Holy One do? God threw truth to the ground and went ahead and created humankind, as it says in Scripture: "You have cast truth to the ground" (Daniel 8:12).
—Genesis Rabba 8:5

PREVARICATION

Zeal for the Truth

Some people gossip out of malice or envy. Our more noble passions can also inspire us to gossip. Zeal for the truth may also move us to reveal unpleasant facts about another person.

What could be more noble than to love truth itself? When we see an unworthy person receiving praise, honor, and rewards, we may feel that we are contributing to a deception unless we reveal the truth. We must then remind ourselves that we are not under any such obligation.

Zeal for Truth Does Not Justify Gossip

It does no harm to think more highly of others than they truly deserve. Our sense of justice may demand that all people receive no more or less than they deserve. Justice must always be tempered by mercy. To grant others more than their due is the essence of grace, charity, and loving-kindness. It is more noble to be gracious than to be truthful. There is a parable that before creating humankind God consulted the angels of all the virtues. Mercy argued in favor of creating humankind. Truth argued against. After hearing all the arguments, God threw truth to the ground and went ahead with the creation of man and woman. The message: we must not second-guess God.

It is true that the world is full of hypocrites who have fooled others into thinking they are capable when they are incompetent, kind when they are cruel, loving when they are selfish, charitable when they are miserly. How often we see unworthy people in high positions! We feel that we can see right through them, and we wonder why everyone doesn't.

God has not appointed us to unmask the hypocrites. We may feel outraged to see falsehood triumph, but if we think about it, we will see that no harm is done to us if others get more than they deserve. There is no maximum quantity of reward in the world which is being cornered by the undeserving. Everyone can get what they deserve and more also, in a loving world. Even if we could make the undeserving sink to their proper level, there is no assurance that the ones who take their place will be any more worthy. For all we know, the person who seems unworthy of receiving reward may have been chosen for some particular reason unknown to you. If replaced, the replacement could be even less deserving. When we gossip against others out of zeal for the truth, there is no assurance that the damage we do to our subject will result in any compensation to the subject's "victims." When passion for truth leads to gossip, no good can come of it, but much harm may be the result.

Arthur is dating Sally. Sally likes to imagine her romances to be more than they sometimes are. Sally tells all the girls that Arthur is dating nobody else but her. Gaile knows for a fact that Arthur is going out with other girls as well.

Gaile likes both Arthur and Sally, but she reveals that Arthur is dating other girls because she wants the truth to be known about the true extent of Arthur's devotion. In her zeal for the truth Gaile hurts Sally's feelings and publicly embarrasses her.

If Gaile believes that Arthur is harming Sally by deliberately leading her on, or that Sally is harming Arthur by falsely claiming him as a boyfriend, then Gaile should rebuke the guilty party in private. If there is no harm to either Sally or Arthur in Sally's fantasy, which is most likely, then there is no need for Gaile to speak up at all.

Carol is always preaching against gambling in any form. Ted sees Carol buying a lottery ticket in the convenience store. He tells others because he just can't bear to see such hypocrisy.

It is gossip for Ted to repeat this to others even if he feels no malice toward Carol.

Ricky happens to know that David got promoted over the other candidates only because the boss thinks David's wife is sweet. Dale came out highest in the competency ratings. Ricky does not really care who got the promotion, but he thinks that everyone should know that Dale earned the highest rating.

Though he is moved only by zeal for the truth, and not out of malice, it would be gossip for Ricky to reveal that Dale outscored David on the ratings.

Everyone thinks that Allen is an honest guy, and indeed he is. Hilary happens to know that when he lived in a another state he was convicted for a variety of fraudulent business practices. It is gossip for Hilary to repeat this fact to everyone, even though her only motive is that no one have misconceptions about Allen.

One must be especially careful about zeal for the truth when speaking about an enemy. Out of zeal for the truth we may want everyone to know the "true evil nature" of our enemy. We may convince ourselves that we are moved only by zeal for the truth, but it is not possible to speak against an enemy without at least a hint of malice. Better to keep silent rather than give in to the desire to make "revelations" about people we do not like.

Beware of statements like the following:

"You all think my ex-husband is so nice? Let me tell you what he is really like . . ."

"You won't think Jill is such a nice person anymore once I tell you all what she did to me last week . . . "

"Anyone who thinks that Dave is a stock market whiz should know what happened to my net worth when I started listening to him . . . "

Statements like these are pure gossip masquerading as the revelation of significant truths.

Unrevealed Misdeeds

You may know that a certain well-respected person has committed a misdeed that is not known to the general public. Your obligation to warn others only applies when you have good reason to believe that a specific harm is about to occur. It is not your task to unmask hidden evildoers. No good can come from the gratuitous revelation of another person's past misdeeds. In this case it is best to leave the truth unknown.

Fairness, Justice, and Mercy

It may be helpful to this discussion to consider the meaning of fairness, justice, and mercy. "Fair" means that everyone gets the same. No one receives more or less than another. "Just" means that everyone gets precisely what they deserve, no more or less. The opposite of "just" is "unjust," in which someone gets less than what is deserved. "Merciful" means everyone gets more than they deserve.

Those who are obsessed with fairness are likely to be opposed to justice, and even more opposed to mercy. It's just not fair for someone to get a higher reward even if it is deserved. It is even more unfair for someone to get more when it is not deserved.

There is no Hebrew word for the concept "fair." The idea of fairness does not even exist in the Bible. The concern for fairness often leads to malicious gossip out of a zeal for truth. The deeper motive is the desire to see that no one receives any more reward or honor than oneself. When we replace a concern for fairness with a concern for justice and mercy, we will always want others to have more honor and reward, never less, regardless of our own status.

Lying

Some people imagine that they excel in the virtue of honesty. They must always speak the truth about what they know and what they feel. May God protect us from such people! There is no measure to the damage they cause in the name of virtue. No obligation exists to spill all of one's knowledge or to reveal all of one's feelings. Honesty in this sense is no virtue at all. The true virtue is to be sensitive and discreet. We can accomplish this by keeping our unflattering feelings and knowledge about others to ourselves except when they must be revealed out of necessity.

"Miriam, I cannot hide my feelings. Your outfit looks hideous."

"Greg, I don't feel right pretending to like my mother-in-law, even though she is your mother and you two are very close. The next time she comes to visit, I'm just going to have to sit her down and tell her what I think of her."

"No, Rob, you were not accepted into the fraternity. I think you should know why. Some of the guys thought that you were a real jerk."

"No, Richie, I will not go out with you. And do you want to know why? Because your ears stick out too far, that's why!"

Some people wrongly believe that "Thou shalt not lie!" is one of the Ten Commandments. Not so! The third commandment obligates us to fulfill vows made in God's name. The ninth commandment prohibits perjury when giving testimony under oath in a court of law. Nowhere in Scripture is there a prohibition of lying. Needless to say, there is no commandment to say what we truly feel out of honesty. In Scripture, silence is always permitted.

Scripture depicts God as telling a lie rather than hurt Abraham's feelings (Genesis 18:13). God reveals to Abraham that he and Sarah are to have a child. Sarah laughs and says, "Shall I have joy now, with my husband so old?" God says to Abraham, "Why did Sarah laugh, saying, 'Shall I have a child when I am so old'?" God changes Sarah's words rather than sow strife between husband and wife.

Lying for the Sake of Peace

One should lie rather than tell the truth when three conditions are met.

1. Your purpose in telling a lie is to create peace between people in a situation where revealing the truth would cause ill feeling.
2. There will be no further consequence to the lie. You will not have to maintain it continuously or tell more lies to maintain the first one. You will not have to "spin the tangled web of the deceiver."
3. You have nothing personal to gain from the lie. Your only intention is to keep the peace.

If you are good with words, and thoughtful, you can often think of a way to avoid talebearing without lying.

"What did the guys think of my play on the basketball court?"

"Ha, ha! Were you hoping there were pro scouts in the audience?"

With this good-natured response you invite your friend to talk about how he feels about his own play, which is much more to the point than what others think, and is probably what he really wanted to discuss in the first place.

When You Are Asked to Give an Opinion

Sometimes friends ask us to give an opinion about an object or service they want to purchase. If your friend has not yet made a commitment to acquire the object or the service, then you may give your honest opinion. If you think the object is inferior in quality or overpriced or frivolous, you may say so.

If your friend has already purchased the article or service in question and merely wants you to confirm the wisdom or good taste of the purchase, it is better not to say what you think. Praise the new acquisition regardless of your true opinion.

"Yes, that dress is lovely."

"You did get a bargain on this used car! You sure know how to deal with those car salespeople!"

And remember, All brides are beautiful on their wedding day! Never, ever give a negative opinion of someone's chosen mate once the die has been cast!

It is always risky to give an honest opinion. Your response may not be what the inquirer wishes to hear. It is best to reserve your honest opinion for matters of fact that are within your expertise, such as quality and price. On matters of taste it is best to say as little as possible unless you are a decorator or fashion consultant who has been hired just for your taste, and even then one must be circumspect. You do not have to answer questions like the following:

"Should I buy a dry wine or a sweet wine?"

"Which looks better on me, the plaid suit or the pinstripe?"

The best answer to such questions is:

"You are so good at choosing! What do you think?"

If you do express an opinion, you should be prepared to have it rejected. Very often people want to hear a contrary opinion just to reject it in order to confirm their own opinion. There is nothing wrong with this. Just because your opinion was solicited does not establish an obligation that it be honored. There is no point in saying:

"Why did you ask my opinion about what to serve if you're not going to listen to me?"

Rather, once your opinion has been rejected, it is gracious to acknowledge the wisdom of your inquirer's own choice.

"Yes, now I see that you are right. It is better to serve fish to that group."

When You Cannot Be Objective

When you are giving your opinion of a possible acquisition, you must be sure that what you say is your true best judgment. If you have a grudge against the seller or you wish to steer someone to another seller, it is best to disqualify yourself from offering an opinion.

"Tell me, I'm thinking of going to Dr. Denton for root canal work. Do you think he's a good dentist?"

"Dr. Florin is one of my best friends and I always go to him. I do not wish to comment on the work of any other dentist."

"Arlene, will I get a good price on a spring dress at Levi's Dress Shop?"

Arlene does not particularly like Mr. Levi, but this is not material to her friend's question. Arlene does not wish to let a personal dislike affect her advice, so she responds, "I really don't know what Levi's is charging, so I am not qualified to tell you. Why don't you check his prices for yourself."

If you know of some objective reason why your friend should not use a particular vendor, then you may give the required warning, but this does not hold in matters of opinion.

When Your Advice Will Not Be Heeded

If you have valid but negative advice and you know that the inquirer will pay no attention to it, then it is preferable to keep silent. It is acceptable to say something bad about some possible acquisition because you want something better for the one who seeks your advice. If you know that the questioner will not respect your opinion, then you are criticizing for no purpose. That turns your advice into malicious gossip.

Henry says to Walter, "Walter, I'm thinking of asking Betty out on a date. She sure is beautiful! What do you think, would she be nice to go out with?" Walter happens to think that for a number of good reasons Betty would be a poor choice for Henry. However, he knows Henry well enough to know that Henry is infatuated and will ask Betty out no matter what he says. Walter therefore says, "Henry, go ahead and follow your heart."

PREJUDICE

Stereotypes: General Comments About Groups or Classes of People

It is wrong to make general evaluative statements about any group or class of people. This is so even when your evaluation is positive. It is a great wrong to make a defamatory evaluative statement about a group or class of people.

Any statement which implies that people act in a certain way or share a certain character trait because of their membership in a group, and not because of their individual choices, is a malicious statement.

Beware of statements like the following:

"All women (Italians, blacks, Jews, WASPs) are . . . "

"All swimmers (fat people, hairdressers, peace marchers) are . . . "

It is equally wrong to judge a group of people whether they are joined by an essential trait, such as race or national origin, or by an incidental trait, such as a chosen profession or being fat or thin or the like.

One may certainly denounce evil traits like hypocrisy, criminality, humorlessness, and laziness, but it is wrong to imply that there is any one identifiable class of people who are more likely to demonstrate this evil trait. Even all those people who do share the trait do not constitute a group. Criticize only the evil trait, not those who possess it. Rather than say *"I do not like lazy people,"* say *"I do not like laziness in people."* Watch out for those who denounce hypocrites as if they constituted an identifiable class of human beings!

Positive stereotypes may seem to be an antidote to negative stereotypes, and therefore good. This is not the case. The goal is to eliminate stereotyping altogether. It is not much of a step for those who believe a positive stereotype about a certain group to accept a negative stereotype as being equally valid.

Someone who says "All Jewish people are smart" might soon be saying, "All Jewish people are cheap."

Someone who says *"Black people are good at sports"* might go on to say *"Black people are not capable of running a business."*

Someone who says *"Italians are good cooks"* may just end up saying *"All Italians are in the Mafia."*

From *"Women are patient"* it is not a big step to say *"Women cannot think as well as men."*

Complimentary stereotypes help to keep minority groups "in their place." Also, members of a minority group who do not fit a positive stereotype that the group holds about itself may feel doubly bad. Imagine an African-American who is not good at basketball. He says to himself, *"Not only do I suffer from racism because I am black, but I don't even succeed as a black person."*

An additional problem with positive stereotypes is that they are like praise spoken in front of a person's enemies. When people mention or hear a complimentary stereotype they are likely to bring up the uncomplimentary ones as well.

In an earlier chapter we discussed the human tendency to rationalize in order to permit gossip, and how these reasons we come up with, however superficially convincing, are not valid. The same applies to repeating stereotypes. They are wrong even if you include yourself or speak about your own group. Jewish humorists who trade in self-stereotypes do much damage to the image of Jews. Though they denigrate only their own group, these humorists are guilty of promoting racist attitudes. Love of neighbor begins with self-love, as it says, "Love your neighbor as yourself" (Leviticus 19:18)

People Are Individuals

Everyone on earth came into being to fulfill a unique purpose that has been granted by God to him or her alone. No human being is quite like any other; none of us shares with anyone else the same unique configuration of life situation, talents, and character. This uniqueness is an important part of what we mean when we say that people are created "in the image of God". Any statement which judges us as a group, whether for good or ill, disparages and diminishes the divine image. Stereotypes are therefore as much an affront against God as against our fellow human beings.

Ethnic Humor

Ethnic jokes are a particularly harmful form of malicious speech. Ethnic jokes generate powerful negative stereotypes about minorities; they are so ubiquitous that it is impossible to avoid them; they are so funny that they are difficult to resist. The mere fact that a stereotype is stated in jest does not make it less damaging. It is even more damaging, since humor provides a shield behind which people feel comfortable promoting ethnic slander.

It takes tremendous self-control to avoid participation in gossip of any kind. The most difficult challenge of all is to resist listening to an ethnic joke that promises to be hilariously funny. Who can withstand the curiosity to find out the punch line? It may be just in response to ethnic humor that the sages of old said: "Who is the true hero? The one who controls his evil impulse" (Avot 4:1).

Listening to Group Slander

Giving ear to a stereotype is as bad as speaking one. Sometimes when people are gossiping one has no choice but to keep silent. Silence is not an adequate response to an ethnic slur. It is a moral obligation to protest against such talk.

It is best to display absolute indignation when you are forced to hear words that malign any group of people. One may say something like the following:

"I beg your pardon, but I resent being subjected to hearing the kind of thing you have just said. As an American I believe in the equality of all people, and I believe in the right of each person to be what he or she wants to be. I simply will not stand still for un-American statements such as what you have just said. Please retract that statement right away."

The great damage caused by ethnic stereotypes obligates us to actively protest against such statements. It is also important to object strongly because those who make derogatory statements against a group will often claim the moral high ground for themselves, citing the supposed faults of the group which they choose to criticize. We must not grant anyone a platform for the spread of ethnic slander.

If someone begins to tell an ethnic joke, it is sufficient to say, "Please stop right there. I do not listen to ethnic humor." You will probably be met with disbelief. "What, you don't want to hear this joke? It's really, really funny." If you are insistent and do not weaken, you will certainly make a great impression on your company. They will observe in your actions a valuable example of ethical behavior.

Certainly you should not go to see a comedy show that is known to include degrading ethnic humor.

The Truth Behind Stereotypes

Some people will defend stereotypes by insisting that they are true. As we have stated above, malicious gossip should not be repeated even if it is true. It is thus immaterial whether an ethnic slur is true or false; it is still absolutely wrong to repeat it. Even so, due to the particularly vicious nature of ethnic stereotypes, it is worth exploring whether they are true or false.

A stereotype is completely true only if it is true of every single member of a group. This is so unlikely that it is a virtual impossibility. Therefore every stereotype is false.

If an ethnic stereotype were true, it would be relevant to ask what makes it true. The wrong behavior that we associate with the members of a particular group has nothing to do with their membership in that group. For instance, there was a high incidence of crime among members of some ethnic groups when they immigrated to America in large numbers at the beginning of the twentieth century. The press and demagogic politicians warned against the "natural criminality" of these ethnic groups, maintaining that they could never be assimilated into decent American society. As the members of these immigrant groups began to meet with economic success, most of the criminals among them disappeared. The seemingly proven association of these ethnic groups with criminal behavior proved to be false. It was only the difficult conditions under which they lived that caused a disproportionate number of them to turn to criminality. In any group of people suffering from poverty and social dislocation, some will turn to criminal activity, though we do not know exactly which ones.

Statistical proofs about the nature of groups are seldom valid because they do not demonstrate any real cause and effect between membership in the group and a particular trait or activity. Statistics are useful for many purposes. Passing judgment on groups of people is not among them. We should leave statistics to sociologists and demographers who are trained to use statistics in objective ways to fulfill legitimate social goals.

Many stereotypes are absolutely false. They are not even statistically valid. For example, there is a stereotype that Jews are cheap, whereas statistics show that Jews, taken as a whole, are among the most generous and charitable of Americans. Once a stereotype has taken hold, it is difficult to convince people of its falsehood, no matter how ridiculous it may be. This is one of the dangers of stereotypes. Even people who try hard not to be prejudiced are likely to harbor a secret notion that what is said about such and such a group is really true. "Where there's smoke, there's fire," they say, to justify clinging to old prejudices

The persistence of certain stereotypes is not a proof that there is any truth in them. Stereotypes acquire their force in the fears and fantasies of those who preserve and repeat them. The truth of a stereotype is to be found in the obsessions of those who repeat them, and not among the innocent victims.

A good example of this is Adolf Hitler. He accused the Jewish people of wanting to control the world. This was a falsehood, but it is clear from Hitler's behavior that he himself desired to control the world. Hitler blamed his victims for "forcing" him to start the Second World War. Many people, unfortunately, have "reasoned" that the Jews must have done something wrong if the Germans hated them so much. Not so! The hatred of the anti-Semite for the Jews says nothing about Jews, but it says worlds about the anti-Semites. If you find yourself prone to believe some particular ethnic stereotype, you might consider inspecting your own soul to discover and root out the source of that belief.

PUBLIC FIGURES

Some people are always in the public eye because their profession makes them well known. Actors and actresses, sports stars and political leaders are in this category, as well as people who are famous in their fields, such as great artists and renowned scientists. Public figures must expect to be subject to public discussion. Celebrity status comes with the territory of being an actor or sports figure, and is helpful in the stars' professional advancement. People come to see sporting events not only because of their interest in the game but because they want to see the celebrities who play it. Actors and actresses are more likely to get good parts if they generate fan enthusiasm. Fans like to come closer to the stars by reading and hearing about their personal lives. Knowing personal news about celebrities makes them seem like members of the family. Many stars encourage this by giving interviews to the press and appearing on television talk shows. The pursuit of personal knowledge about stars and celebrities whom you admire is not gossip.

In the case of political leaders, it is necessary for the public to know enough about their personal lives so that we will be able to evaluate their character. It is the duty of good citizens to know about the public and private lives of their elected leaders. Anyone who runs for office in a free, democratic country must be prepared to live under public scrutiny. There may be a line, though, which journalists should not cross in respecting the privacy of political leaders. It is hard to generalize about what matters the public needs to know in the private lives of their elected leaders. This is a matter of constant debate, as it probably ought to be.

There is a branch of journalism that specializes in spreading malicious gossip about celebrities. This type of writing does not encourage the adulation of fans. It appeals to the popular taste for gossip, the desire to observe the downfall of the high and mighty. Celebrities justly feel hurt by the outrageous allegations made against them in the tabloid newspapers and magazines. It is not proper to read this kind of gossipy journalism or to repeat the allegations one finds there. One might say, "What can it hurt such famous people for me to repeat rumors about them? They don't know or care what I think anyway. I don't really believe the gossip columnists; I just enjoy reading what they have to say." We must remember that celebrities also have human feelings. They are hurt when nasty rumors about them are made public. It might take them many years to live down a slanderous allegation. Also, reading tabloid newspapers encourages our own taste for gossip, which is not healthy for us.

PROMISES

The Sanctity of Oral Contracts

Once one has given verbal agreement to a contract, one is absolutely obligated to fulfill it in every aspect. It is of no consequence whether you have shaken hands or signed a written contract or in any other way formalized your agreement. Your word alone should be all that is necessary to seal any deal.

Modern society has become paper crazy. Technology has made it easy to generate documents. We have become dependent upon paper contracts in the conduct of our business. Documents are valuable up to a point, but lawyers will tell you that it is impossible to write out an agreement so fully that the terms cannot be disputed. It takes the good will and faithfulness of all parties to make a bargain hold. A verbal agreement should be considered as binding as a thousand-page contract in fine print that has been inspected by an army of lawyers. This is so even if you later have second thoughts or realize that you could have made a better deal. Jewish tradition illustrates this principle with a story.

A certain wealthy man wishes to buy a precious jewel. He hears that a Jewish gem dealer is currently in possession of a particularly fine stone. The wealthy man goes to the home of the Jewish dealer at the moment that he is reciting his evening prayers. The prospective buyer is welcomed into the home by the dealer's child. The man sees the dealer standing in the corner of the back room. "I will pay you a thousand dinars for the jewel in your possession," the wealthy man shouts. The child says to the man, "Please do not speak to my father now. He is occupied." Since the dealer is alone, the wealthy man assumes that he is coyly holding out for a higher price. "All right," he says, "I will pay you two thousand dinars if you will give me that precious stone." The dealer concludes his prayers and turns his attention to his customer. "I could not interrupt my prayers," he says, "but when I heard you offer a thousand dinars for this jewel I accepted your offer in my heart. As far as I am concerned, our deal was concluded at that point. I cannot abuse my prayers by accepting your second, higher offer. The jewel is yours for a thousand dinars."

In a country where there is an old-fashioned bazaar, one can see the difference between American society and a traditional society which still takes verbal commitments seriously. There is an etiquette to the bazaar and a sense of honor which Americans may not recognize in their worry over whether they are getting the best price or being treated as suckers. The shopkeepers in the bazaar will bargain hard and use every psychological trick to get the highest price from you, but once they have committed themselves to a sale they will not retract. In the heat of bargaining they sometimes get carried away and offer to sell something for less than it costs them, but they will not retract. It is hard for them to understand what is lacking in their American customers, who will offer a price for an item, and if the dealer accepts it will often try to get a still lower price. This tendency to take our word lightly is one of the things that makes American tourists unpopular in foreign countries. We should recognize that honoring a verbal commitment is more important than driving a hard bargain.

Every Word a Promise

If you are careful to fulfill your every word, then your word—even your most casual statement—always has the force of a solemn oath. If your word has this power, you will never have to swear an oath. Many religious people are very careful about this matter, in respect to truthfulness and also in respect to the many warnings in Scripture against swearing oaths. They recognize that guilt is incurred by one who swears an oath and then is unable to fulfill it.

In the year 1240 Rabbi Yehiel of Paris was ordered to defend Judaism in a mock trial for the amusement of Queen Blanche of France. A Hebrew transcript of the proceedings has come down to us (in *Otzar Havikuhim*). The queen ordered Rabbi Yehiel to be sworn in. The honor of Judaism and the future of French Jewry were at stake. One would think that in this situation Rabbi Yehiel would not risk antagonizing the queen in any way. Yet Rabbi Yehiel refused to take the oath. He spent the whole first day of the trial pleading before Queen Blanche to allow his testimony to stand for itself, for never in his whole life had he sworn an oath. After the trial the Talmud was condemned—a foregone conclusion—but Rabbi Yehiel maintained his integrity, and his example inspired the Jews of France in those difficult times.

The state generally requires the swearing of an oath when one testifies in court or applies for various types of licenses. Several states respect the religious scruple that makes some people reluctant to swear an oath. In West Virginia, for example, witnesses giving testimony are requested to swear "or affirm" that their statement is true.

Never swear an oath in ordinary conversation. It may be unavoidable to swear an oath when testifying in court, but there is no need to swear to attest to the veracity of one's ordinary statements. If you make a habit of saying "Swear to God" or "Cross my heart" or "May so-and-so happen to me if this is not true," you may end up swearing such oaths even to exaggerated claims or unprovable contentions. If someone asks you to swear in ordinary conversation, respond, "My word is sufficient." Hopefully this is true; and if not, your oath will not improve matters much.

Every Word a Solemn Promise

The way to avoid swearing oaths is to treat every single word you say as a solemn promise. People should know that if you say you will do something, you will. If you say something will happen, it will happen. If you say something is a fact, it is. Then, even if you say something nearly incredible, people will believe you.

It is a great benefit to go through life with a reputation for veracity. In order to acquire such a reputation, you must watch your words at all times. You must be sure never to exaggerate your statements. You must be careful never to make idle promises or idle threats that you have no intention of fulfilling. If you wish to speak of a doubtful matter or a matter of opinion, preface your remarks with "I believe" or "It may be." Avoid all-inclusive statements. Any statement that begins with "all people" or "always" or "in every case" is likely to be false, and it is best to think twice before using such expressions.

Promises to Children

One should be especially careful about promises to children. We so often make false promises to children, just to silence them. Children quickly come to realize that their parents' promises mean very little. Such experiences train children from the very beginning to discount the value of words.

"Not now, Benny, but we can go to Disney World next year if you're good."

Fine, but only if you really intend to go and you are pretty sure that the trip is possible for you.

"If you will stop crying now I'll buy you an ice cream on the way home."

Do not say this for the sake of a momentary respite in the hope that your child will forget about your promise. Even if the child forgets, you should remember.

"Wake up! It's time for that ice cream I promised you. Remember?"

Idle threats are a common form of false promise. Parents often make exaggerated threats in exasperation. A threat is a form of oath and should be fulfilled. We must be very careful, then, about how we threaten our children. Here are some threats that should never be spoken:

"I'll kill you if you do that one more time."

"One more bad report card and I will ground you forever. You'll never see the light of day again."

"If you don't eat your peas you will have to go right to bed" (when you have no intention of expending the energy it would take to fulfill this threat).

A proper threat to a child is a dispassionate statement of the consequences that will follow upon improper action. The punishment should be proportionate to the wrong and of a limited duration. It should be a threat that you are perfectly willing and able to carry out. For example:

"If you do that again you will spend an hour in your room and miss your favorite TV show."

"If your grades do not improve you will be restricted from phone calls for two hours every weekday evening."

Threats like these are easy to carry out if necessary. Your children will then learn two good lessons—that every act has its consequence, and that their parents' word is their bond. Your children will learn the importance of keeping one's word by your example.

The Sanctity of a Sworn Oath

While it is better never to swear an oath, if you do swear one you must treat it with the greatest sanctity. If you have sworn upon the name of God, you are obligated by the third of the Ten Commandments, "You shall not take the name of Adonai your God in vain."

One should swear by the name of God only if one truly believes in God. A nonbeliever may not believe in the existence of a God whose name can be desecrated, but he is still under an ethical obligation not to recite an oath that, for him, would be a vain oath. According to Jewish teaching, one should not swear by the name of any other god. One should swear only in the manner approved by one's own religion. One should swear a formal oath only in a manner not contradictory to one's own religion.

A true story:

I went to the courthouse with my fiancée to get a marriage license. The county clerk attempted to swear me in. I explained that I would prefer not to swear. The clerk explained that she was only doing her job—no oath, no license. There being no possibility of appeal, I agreed to be sworn in. The county clerk took out of her desk a Bible containing the New Testament. Since I am Jewish and do not believe in the New Testament as sacred Scripture, I asked to have a copy of the Old Testament only upon which to swear. The clerk searched the whole courthouse and did not find any other Bible. Mine was the first such request ever, explained the clerk by way of apology. For lack of a better solution, I opened the book between the Old and New Testaments and swore on the Old Testament side.

It made me sad to think how many non-Christians had sworn falsely on that New Testament, and how the bureaucrats insisted on an oath but did not care at all whether the form of the oath was true or false. When oaths were taken seriously, the oath of a Jew was not accepted unless it was made upon a Torah scroll, as is proper.

If there is so little respect for the sanctity of oaths, why require them at all? Will a person who swears on a book of unknown content speak the truth out of fear of blaspheming the name of God within the book?

PROFANITY

One should studiously avoid the use of profanity, whether in the form of obscene oaths, foul words, or crude suggestions. Profanity devalues speech. It insults the human dignity of those who speak it and those who listen to it.

Another true story:

When I was in college I joined the fencing club. One day after practice I was changing in the locker room along with one of my clubmates. I mentioned to him that I had gone out on a date the previous Saturday night. He responded with a comment of an obscene sexual nature. I ignored the comment, which I dismissed as typical locker room talk. I was surprised when my partner immediately blushed and apologized. "I'm sorry," he said, "I didn't mean to imply anything about you or the lady, or your relationship with her. I hope I have not offended you."

Truth to tell, I had not been offended. I expected to hear such crude talk in a locker room. Though not offended, I found myself greatly honored that my friend considered me to be a person of such sensitivity and high ideals, and such refinement, that I would be offended by an obscene innuendo.

As days passed I found that the memory of my friend's apology remained with me. It continued to make me feel good about myself. I then made a commitment to myself never again to use obscene language in the presence of others. If it is so easy to compliment other people at no cost to myself, then I would be foolish not to take advantage of this opportunity.

As my friend's sensitivity made me feel good about myself, it also filled me with admiration for him. What an easy way to win admiration—just refrain from using obscene language! Besides, profanities have long lost their shock value. If one wishes to use words to grab attention and express strong feeling, a string of profanities will no longer do it. A statement of strong feeling that is devoid of vain oaths will be more noticeable and will make the point more effectively. Your listeners will be shocked to hear you speak strongly without profanity, and will take your words more seriously. Even your insults (God forbid) will sting more if spoken with wit instead of profanity.

Obscene talk reveals the speaker as vulgar and unimaginative. Sometimes people wish to come across this way in order to make it clear that they are not snobs or effete intellectuals. Even such individuals may find that the opportunity to win the admiration of others while helping them to feel good about themselves is reason enough to refrain from using profane speech.

Chapter 6
When You Are a Victim of Hatred or Rebuke

> Do not rebuke a scoffer, for he will hate you. Reprove a wise person and he will love you.
> —Proverbs 9:8

> It is shocking to see a person deliberately destroy a thing of value. There is nothing more valuable than a human being, and nothing more damaging than gossip.
> —*Shemirat Halashon*

THE POWER OF WORDS

Gossip does a lot of damage. Gossip deeply hurts the feelings of its victims. A nasty rumor may cause material damage, even to the point of ruin. A person's livelihood or happiness can be destroyed by a few ill-considered words.

Fortunately, situations in which gossip alone causes grave injury are rare. If you are honest in business, your reputation among your many satisfied customers will usually outbalance the rumors started by the one bad customer who carries an open grudge against you. If you live with integrity, it is unlikely that enough people would accept a false rumor about you to permanently block your advancement toward a chosen objective. Most of the time our deeds speak for themselves, protecting us from material harm due to the words of others. Ironically, when someone is destroyed by a false rumor, it is often because the allegation touches painfully close to his or her faults. Everything we do, say, think, and feel, whether for good or for bad, comes back upon us in some way in equal measure.

We must know how to respond when we are threatened, hurt, or exposed to ridicule by malicious gossip. How can we defend ourselves without looking even more ridiculous, and without falling to the level of our accusers?

HUMILITY

Humility is the best cure for hurt feelings caused by gossip. One who develops genuine humility will realize that the praise and admiration of society is not a right. Admiration is a gift which we must not expect, even when we deserve more than we get. A person strong in humility cannot be humiliated. Gossip hurts only the gossiper. It cannot take away from us anything that belongs to us by right.

The humble person is able to see from more than one perspective. Our suffering at the hands of a gossiper may be justified between us and God, even if it is unjust from the perspective of the gossiper. A false accusation may be seen from one perspective as a golden opportunity to test our humility, to see whether we care too much for the opinion of others, or whether we are content to be satisfied with our own clear conscience.

From the attitude of humility we will see that no person has the power to do us any harm with words. We will come to see that any anger that we feel toward gossipers is due only to a point of view that we do not have to take. We can just as easily adopt a perspective from which it seems that we have suffered no harm. A gnat seems important to itself, but to a person on a mission the buzzing gnat is too insignificant to notice. So it is with the humble person and the habitual gossiper.

From the attitude of humility there is a good thing to say whenever we hear that someone has gossiped against us:

"If he knew my other faults he would have mentioned them as well."

It may seem as if this response will have the undesirable effect of validating the malicious allegations that have been made against you. Would it not be more honest, more just, more dignified, to deny the allegations? Logically, these objections make sense. But here we must be ruled not by cold logic but by the nature of the human heart. One who has heard both the words of your slanderer and your response will judge between you by the relative quality of character that you both display. The more you raise your voice in anger and righteous indignation, the more people will be inclined to believe the reports against you. If you display humility and equanimity, others will be so impressed with your forbearance that they will be inclined to disbelieve or excuse any uncomplimentary report about you. Your humility will be measured against the obvious malice of the gossiper. "If he knew my other faults he would have mentioned them as well." Strange though it seems, the more you say this, the more others will insist that you are innocent of faults.

There is a wonderful paradox in humility. The more you develop it, the greater you will seem in the eyes of others. There was a Hasidic rabbi who understood this paradox well. He used to tell everyone, "I am one of the most exceedingly humble people you will ever meet."

There is a wonderful phrase in the prayer of the talmudic sage Mar bar Ravina, a prayer which is recited thrice daily in the Jewish liturgy. The phrase is, *"May my soul seem as dust to everyone."* If you will meditate on this one phrase every morning before you start your day, then nothing anyone says to you or about you during the day will hurt you. If people speak ill of you, it will not matter to you. If they speak well of you, you will be as pleasantly surprised as if your friends gave you a surprise party on your birthday. Is this not a more pleasant way to go through life than with constant feelings of anger and depression because others are not granting you your due?

With the attitude of humility you will realize that when people gossip against you they are causing trouble only to themselves. You will feel sorry for them. If someone should come to you as a talebearer, you will respond with pity for the one who gossiped against you.

IF YOU ARE ACCUSED OF AN IMMORAL ACT

What we have said above applies whenever you have been criticized for your faults. Humility permits us to admit to faults, whether or not we are guilty of them. One should not admit to having committed immoral deeds or criminal acts. To do so would create an injustice against ourselves and undermine the example we hope to set by our actions. The best response to a false accusation of immorality is, "I regret that so-and-so has chosen to accuse me." It is not necessary to excuse or explain oneself beyond this. The charges will soon fly away of their own weightlessness.

If an unknown person has committed some wrongful act and you are among the suspects, it is sufficient to say, "I am not the one who did it." There is no need to speculate on the likely perpetrator.

LOVING REBUKE

Most of use find it difficult to accept criticism. We become defensive in the face of rebuke. We leap to justify ourselves. We shut off our minds and do not let any words of criticism enter our ears. Rebuke is hard to take when it comes from a person in authority—a boss or a teacher or a leader. It is even harder to accept rebuke from a peer—a co-worker or a friend or a sibling. It is nearly unbearable to accept rebuke from a subordinate, an employee, or a child.

The wise overcome their human nature and train themselves to love rebuke. One can learn a lot from rebuke, whether spoken in anger or out of genuine concern. We might learn some way that we can improve ourselves. Even a tongue-lashing from a spiteful person may contain some surprising insight into our character that we can use to our own advantage if we will only listen.

Rabbi Yohanan ben Nuri said: "Many times Rabbi Akiva was whipped on account of me, when I complained about him, by order of Rabban Gamaliel (the president of the high court of rabbis), but I know that Akiva loved me all the more on that account, to fulfill the word of Scripture, 'Rebuke a wise man and he will love you' (Proverbs 9:8)" (Sifra to Leviticus 89a–b).

GIVING REBUKE

It is a moral obligation to rebuke someone who you believe has wronged you. This may seem surprising. One might think that a saintly person would overlook a wrong and just forget about it, rather than deliver a rebuke. On deeper consideration we see that it is virtually impossible to totally forget a slight. Unless the wound is treated it will become infected. The pain of feeling victimized might fester into hatred unless it is properly disposed of. Rather than trust yourself to be a saint, learn the proper way to give a rebuke. This means that you must be ready to be appeased by the person who wronged you. Maybe he or she did not realize you were being wronged or saw the act in a different light than you. Maybe there were circumstances of which you are unaware. Maybe he or she did harm you intentionally, but is now ready to undo the wrong and return to friendship. You will never know unless you first deliver a rebuke.

The biblical verse "You shall love your neighbor as yourself" (Leviticus 19:18) is often identified as the ethical commandment which includes all others. In the preceding verse we are commanded "You shall surely rebuke your neighbor, and not bear sin on his account." The association of these verses is no accident. If you will rebuke your neighbor, you will love your neighbor, but if you will not rebuke your neighbor, you will not love your neighbor.

A proper rebuke is spoken without anger, hatred, or malice, but only for the sake of undoing a wrong and improving the subject's future deeds.

If your words of rebuke are overly harsh, they may cause the subject to blush with shame or turn pale with embarrassment. The Jewish sages compared this to shedding the blood of the innocent. Your words must be sufficiently gentle that they do not cause any change in your subject's demeanor.

The person you rebuke must know that you have his or her best interests at heart. If your manner of speaking is such that he or she is able to truly listen to you, only then can it be said that you have delivered a rebuke as commanded in Leviticus 19.

A proper rebuke cannot be delivered in the heat of anger. If you are angry, delay until your anger has passed. Then go to rebuke your neighbor.

Those who do not rebuke the subject of their anger are likely to pour out their wrath through gossip. If you are displeased with the actions of another person, above all do not tell a third party. Tell only the person who has displeased you, using gentle words of rebuke. If you are skilled at delivering a rebuke, you will be less likely to resort to gossip when you are angry or hurt.

REVENGE

The Bible says, "Vengeance is mine, says Adonai" (Deuteronomy 32:35). This verse has been misused to imply that the God of the Bible is vengeful. The true meaning of the verse is that vengeance belongs to God, who is always merciful, and never to human beings who may be lacking in mercy. One should not take private vengeance in any form, even if there is no other way to get justice. Better for the perpetrator to go unpunished than for you to endanger your soul with an act of vengeance.

Revenge is not a justification for gossip. We have no special permission to gossip against others to punish them for wrongs committed against ourselves.

Jewish tradition permits the public shaming of known evildoers, in order to publicize the negative consequences of evil. If this permission is at all valid in today's world, it certainly does not apply to someone who has wronged you personally. That would be taking vengeance, not hating evil.

Leviticus 19:18 reads in full: *"You shall not take vengeance or bear a grudge against your neighbor. You shall love your neighbor as yourself. I am Adonai."*

What is the difference between taking vengeance and bearing a grudge? Jewish tradition gives us this insight (Sifra to Leviticus 19):

Vengeance is: You ask your neighbor to lend you his axe and he refuses. Later he asks to borrow your hoe and you say to him, "Since you did not lend me your axe, I will not lend you my hoe."

Bearing a grudge is: You ask your neighbor to lend you his axe and he refuses. Later he asks to borrow your hoe and you say to him, "Sure you can borrow my hoe, because I am not like you."

The proper response to the neighbor who borrows but will not lend is to say with a cheerful countenance, in all sincerity, "Certainly, I am happy to lend you my hoe." This is what it is to love one's neighbor. What your neighbor would do if the situation were reversed is irrelevant. It is only important for you to do what is right. The task of the individual is to act with love at all times, not to be a rod of justice.

You may fear that others will take advantage of you if you refuse to play tit for tat. Fear not! You are not a sucker if you always do what is right and good. If anyone comes to think of you as an easy touch and imagines that he is taking advantage of you, that is his own problem. You are giving your love for free. That being the case, you could hardly be underpaid for it.

CRIMES

If a crime has been committed against you, you may report it to the police. If you have suffered monetary damages at the hands of another, you may bring a civil suit. Bringing a person to court is not considered vengeful. Just the opposite; going to court is what we are supposed to do instead of taking vengeance. A properly constituted court is God's representative on earth. Its judgments are God's judgments, and its punishments are God's just retribution. The practical meaning of "*Vengeance is mine, says Adonai*" is that we should take legal action in court against those against whom we have complaints.

THE ROD OF DIVINE JUSTICE

Hillel the Elder found a skull floating down a stream. He picked it up and said to it, "Because you drowned others, you were drowned, and those who drowned you shall also drown" (Avot 2:6).

The sages asked, "If God's providence is over all God's creatures, why does Scripture command us to build a parapet for our roof? If it be God's will, the one on the roof will fall, and if not, then not." They answered, "Even if this is true, when God desires to punish an evil person, God chooses an evil person to carry out the punishment" (Sifrei, Deut. 229).

You may be tempted to take vengeance not out of any personal enmity toward a wrongdoer, but out of a noble passion for justice. As we have seen, a noble impulse may serve as well as a selfish impulse to bring about an evil result. It is necessary to train all one's impulses, good and bad, toward the service of goodness. The sages taught that the person who serves as the rod of God's justice was not chosen for this role as a reward for righteousness, but as a punishment for wickedness. The one who serves as God's rod of justice will himself be brought to account for taking vengeance. If you imagine to yourself that you are doing God's work in publicizing the evil deeds of wrongdoers, you might be right—but if you are right, woe to you! It is not something to brag about, but to be ashamed of. If there is someone who deserves to be exposed and punished for wronging you, you should pray that when the punishment finally comes, you have nothing to do with it. If you remember this, you will not be tempted to respond improperly to hatred and verbal abuse.

THE POLITE WAY TO TAKE REVENGE

Miss Manners, the etiquette advisor, is the literary persona of Judith Martin. Those who wish to become expert at the proper use of speech would do well to familiarize themselves with her newspaper column and books.

Miss Manners often receives letters from her "Gentle Readers" asking how best to respond to some social slight. The tone of these letters makes it clear that what the Gentle Reader wants from Miss Manners is permission to take vengeance and a recommendation of the best way to go about it. The Gentle Reader desires from Miss Manners a witty and devastating response which will repay the affront.

Miss Manners always replies that the correct response to a social insult is to not respond at all. One should be correct in every way and seem not to notice that any insult was intended or given.

We learn from Miss Manners not only that it is proper to refrain from taking vengeance, but that even from the perspective of getting even, not taking vengeance is the best vengeance. If some social rival really did intend to insult you, responding in kind will only fill your rival with glee, while good manners and kindliness will be infuriating and frustrating beyond measure. Besides, someone must take the first step in raising the general level of social behavior. If you desire to teach someone a lesson, make it a lesson in good manners!

MEASURE FOR MEASURE

The righteous do not forbear vengeance because they believe that wrongs should go unpunished. On the contrary, they forbear vengeance because they believe that wrongs do not go unpunished. They have faith that every wrong deed brings its own punishment in its wake. The Jewish sages taught: "Every good deed is its own reward, and every bad deed is its own punishment" (Avot 4:2).

In Jewish tradition there is a principle called "measure for measure": "As you measure out, so shall it be measured unto you" (Sanhedrin 100a). Similar is the Eastern religious concept of karma, the belief that by your deeds you create the aura in which you live your life. Those who do good are rewarded with a good karma, while those who do wrong are punished by their bad karma.

The belief in measure for measure does not mean that if you do right you will receive a material reward in life. It does not mean that good people will prevail over bad people. Common sense and experience tell us that life does not work this way. The belief in measure for measure, rather, informs us that even if our enemies should overcome us with their unethical methods, they will not enjoy their victory. In some proportionate way they will suffer for their actions. And we, if we stick to the right path, will end up happier than if we had lowered ourselves to the level of our enemies in order to vanquish them.

Rick was envious of Darren for having such a beautiful girlfriend, Valerie. Rick used every trick to try to steal Valerie away from Darren. He eventually succeeded. Darren was heartbroken for quite some time, but then he met Rachel, who really loved him, and he ended up as happy as could be. Rick found that having Valerie as a girlfriend was not as exciting as trying to steal her from Darren. Much to his disappointment, he still felt empty of love.

BE SELFISH!

You have a right to take care of your own soul, even if it means that justice will not be done. Those who harm you also harm their own spiritual well-being. If you take vengeance to exact retribution, you will create a devastating disturbance in the peace of your own soul. Be a little selfish! Take care of yourself, and let justice take care of itself!

EXPRESSING ANGER

There are those who will teach you that unexpressed anger will harm your psyche. "Anger should never be held in," they say. Those who say this are wrong! The truth is that anger is always hard to handle, but only when anger is expressed in words or deeds does it damage the psyche.

A boiler without a steam valve might explode, destroying the boiler and damaging everything near it. You must open a valve to let off steam.

This is the analogy used to justify verbalizing anger, and we call it "letting off steam." This analogy is not accurate or useful, because humans do not respond to feelings of anger the way boilers respond to steam pressure. Just the opposite. With humans, letting off steam creates more pressure, not less.

The more you express your anger, the more anger you will feel. Think about your own experiences and you will see that this is true. When you vent your anger toward another person in hard words, the deep wells of anger within you increase their flow. In the end you feel more angry than before. The release and satisfaction that you had hoped for elude you. Your tantrum accomplishes nothing for you, does not have the desired effect upon the subject of your anger, and makes everyone around you think less of you instead of your subject.

The way to overcome anger is to hold it in.

Wait for the storm to blow over before setting sail! Calm yourself down, and do not speak about the subject of your anger until you are calm. Count to ten, a thousand times! Then, instead of expressing anger, give a proper and gentle rebuke. You will feel better, and your gentle words may even accomplish what you wanted to but could not accomplish with your anger.

Dina was so angry with Paul that she felt she would explode. When she saw Paul with some of his friends at the mall, she said to herself, "Here's my chance to show him up for what he really is in front of everyone." Dina ran up to Paul and began to berate him. There is no bad thing that she did not call him. Paul just stood there in silence, feeling embarrassed but not knowing how to respond to this unexpected outburst. When Dina spent her anger she went away. Getting into her car, she was surprised to see that she could hardly hold the steering wheel, her arms were trembling so with anger. Funny, she thought she had gotten her anger out, but now she was more angry than ever. Yelling at Paul felt good at the time, but in retrospect it did not give her the satisfaction she thought it would. She felt as if she hadn't said what she really wanted to say. She felt as if she had been punished more than Paul. Meanwhile, back at the mall, Paul's friends commiserated with him. "What a hothead that Dina is!" said one. "Wow! I guess that was today's entertainment!" said another. Paul was relieved to see that none of his friends seemed to have heard any of the accusations Dina had leveled against him. He soon felt normal again. "Why did Dina make such a fool of herself?" he asked himself in wonder.

If your feelings are so strong that you are not able to withhold your anger, follow this old trick: write down every angry thing you want to say and mail it in a letter to yourself. When you receive the letter, read it and then throw it in the trash!

A HARD DECISION

The following is a true story. Names and circumstances have been changed to protect the innocent.

Sam and Ned were partners in a business. They had a falling out and went their separate ways. Sam kept the business, while Ned entered a different one.

Sometime later a group of Sam's business competitors came to him in great agitation. "Ned is saying things to people that will undermine us all and damage our whole industry," they told him. "Nobody can stop Ned but you. You have to save us, please!"

Due to various circumstances, only Sam could stop Ned. He could make public certain facts from his former business relationship with Ned that would destroy Ned's credibility. If Sam were to do this, Ned would be ruined. He would never again be able to make a living.

This was very tempting for Sam. He was being asked to destroy his enemy Ned—not out of hatred and envy, not to bring retribution for the way Ned had treated him, but in order to save a group of innocent people who had come to him for help. Sam had a moral obligation to help his business competitors. Why should they suffer just because Ned was getting even with Sam?

Sam wanted to help his innocent competitors, but he had a problem. Sam was always careful to observe the rules against gossip. He knew that if he exposed Ned in order to save his competitors, he would of necessity take pleasure in hurting his enemy. Sam knew that this would be bad for him. How could he measure his obligation to preserve the purity of his own soul against his obligation to the people in his business?

In the end, Sam decided not to expose Ned. He and his competitors would just have to suffer through Ned's insults and hope that the damage to them was not too severe. Sam could not allow himself to be the cause of his enemy's downfall.

WHAT THEY SAY, WHAT YOU SAY

As you go through life, it is inevitable that you will make some people angry. You may anger someone by accident, without realizing what you were doing. Or you may anger someone as you walk with integrity, regretfully acknowledging that others will be upset with you for your actions. Whether you anger someone accidentally or knowingly, you must be prepared for the possibility that this person will not be able to withhold anger or refrain from gossiping against you. You must be prepared to listen to a scathing rebuke. You must be prepared for the possibility that this person will tell everyone about the terrible thing you did, putting it in the worst possible light and misrepresenting your motives. In short, you may anger someone who is not as careful as you about the rules of proper speech. But such people are not "outside the tribe." You owe them the same respect that you owe to those who are wise in matters of the tongue.

When this happens to you, please remember this important rule, which may be the most valuable piece of advice in this book:

What others say about you in anger has no power to harm you. What you say in reply does have the power to harm you.

No matter what mean or cruel things someone says to you in rebuke, he or she will not hold these things against you once no longer angry—indeed, will probably not even remember saying these things. A rebuker who was your friend before will be your friend again. A rebuker who admired you before will admire you again, maybe even more so on account of your reticence.

If you become angry or defensive and respond, even if only to defend and explain your actions, your words will be remembered against you. All the more will this be true if you respond in kind to an improper rebuke. After they cool down, those who rebuke you will forget what they said to you, but they will never forget what you said to them. You risk making permanent enemies by responding in kind. Even if a person is not to your liking, what benefit is there to you in gaining an enemy? It is not worth the meager satisfaction of an angry response, which will, in any event, only increase your inner feelings of anger and outrage.

It often happens that hours or days after receiving an angry rebuke you suddenly think of some clever or humiliating response that might have turned the tables. You say to yourself, "How come I can never think of these things at the right time?" You imagine how different matters would have been if only you had been quick with a comeback.

Do not worry about your lack of quick wit. It was an angel from heaven who impeded your timely response, perhaps as a reward for some unacknowledged good deed. Your witless silence preserved you from endless trouble.

A person who is angry with you may gossip about you. Some talebearer is sure to bring you a report of what was said. If you respond in kind, the same talebearer will bring your angry response back to the person who is angry with you. Then that person will surely become your enemy. He or she will no longer remember what you did to make him angry, but will always remember what you said about him in response to his gossip against you. To prevent this escalating cycle of nastiness, it is best to say something like this when a talebearer brings you a report of someone who is gossiping against you out of anger:

"I am sorry to hear that Janet is angry with me. I hope that in time she will forgive me."

"Bob and I had an honest disagreement over that issue. I cannot change my mind about what I did, but I do hope that Bob will

come to see that I did not intend to insult him by not taking his advice."

Notice that the speakers do not address the issue at all, but only the feelings of anger. They say nothing critical about the other person. They are sympathetic toward his or her anger. (After all, anger is a character weakness in the angry person. You should be as sympathetic to such a weakness as you would be toward a friend who is disabled by an illness.)

You need not fear that if you do not defend yourself others will believe what was said about you in anger. When an angry person speaks, no one hears what is said. All that people hear is the anger. They will come away from hearing a critical speech against you and will conclude to themselves simply that "so-and-so is certainly angry." Some habitual gossiper who overhears the angry statement might use it against you, but that should not be a great worry for you and should not be held against the friend who let anger temporarily overcome good sense.

In the face of anger and rebuke you can never fail by keeping silent. Silence will never be held against you. Remember what they said about the fish: if he had kept his mouth shut, he would not have been hooked.

If you follow this advice you will never lose a friend and you will never make an enemy.

Chapter 7
Secrets

> A base person gives away secrets, but a trustworthy soul keeps a confidence.
> —Proverbs 11:13

WHAT IS A SECRET?

Every personal communication must be considered a secret. It is not necessary for the speaker to say, "This is a secret." Clearly, if someone tells you something and then says, "This is a secret; don't tell anyone!" you must keep what he said to yourself. This is equally true of any personal revelation granted to you in private conversation with another person. If someone says something personal or about another person to you alone, or to you and one other person in your company, then you must consider the communication a secret, and you must keep it to yourself.

One should not reveal a secret to anyone.

There is an important exception to this rule, which we have already mentioned in another chapter. If someone tells you that he is abusing a child, physically or sexually, or intends to do physical harm to himself or another person, you must go to the proper authorities and tell them what you have heard.

All of these statements should be considered secrets:

"Ken, I think I'm in love with Martha."

"Nothing's been formally announced yet, but I'm as good as appointed the new district manager for the Northeast."

"Yesterday I didn't feel well."

"I happen to know that Althea has been diagnosed with cancer."

It may seem that there is nothing wrong with repeating these statements. They contain news that seems to be good, or that we may wish to act upon with congratulations or consolation. Still, these are private revelations. It is best to consider them secrets unless you have specific permission from the concerned parties to repeat the information to others.

BEFORE THREE

According to traditional Jewish wisdom, a communication addressed to three or more people is not considered a secret. If you are in the company of four or more people, and one of the group reveals a personal matter, you are free to repeat it to others. You may assume that since the matter was spoken before a group, the teller does not mind if the information is repeated. This permission is not valid, of course, if the speaker announces that "this is a secret."

Alberta announces at her weekly bridge party, "Martin and I are getting a divorce." Since she told this before the seven other people at the bridge party, they are free to repeat it to others, unless Alberta says something like "please do not repeat this to anyone until you see the legal notice in the newspaper."

One should not repeat the information if it is gossip—that is, a matter which lowers your subject in the esteem of others. You may only repeat information which it would be permissible to speak if it came first from your own lips.

The permission to repeat information only holds if there are at least three listeners. If two people tell a matter to two others, there are only two listeners. The communication is then considered a private message. The two listeners must treat the information as a secret. They are not free to repeat it.

There is one important exception to the rule that "three people make a company." *If one of the three listeners is known to be free of gossip, that listener does not count as one of the three.* If a matter is heard by two ordinary people and one who is known never to engage in gossip, it is as if the matter were spoken before only two. Telling a matter to one who does not gossip is like "talking to a wall or a tree." *The same exception holds true if someone repeats information before three others, but one or more of the listeners are relatives or dear friends of the subject.* We are free to assume that people do not spread information about relatives or dear friends. For the purposes of this particular revelation, the friends and relatives are like people who never gossip.

REPEATING A MATTER HEARD IN A GROUP

Someone who hears a matter that is revealed before a company of people is free to repeat the matter to you. If you are not in a company when you hear the information, you may not pass it along. You must treat it as a secret from the person who revealed it to you, even though that person is free to repeat the information to anyone. This rule is not changed if the person who tells you gives you explicit permission to repeat the information. Only the original speaker may give such permission.

Allen tells everyone in his bowling league that he will soon be moving to Albuquerque. Jonathan, who is on Allen's bowling team, repeats this information in private conversation with his friend Rob. Jonathan may repeat the information to whomever he wishes, but Rob should treat the information as a secret, since he was told by Jonathan in a private conversation.

INFORMATION WHICH IS OPEN TO INTERPRETATION

Many statements about others can be interpreted either in a positive light or in a negative light, depending upon the perspective of the speaker. If such matters are told to you in private, you should not repeat them, just in case the speaker had a negative intention. If the same thing is told to you as a member of a group of three or more, you are permitted to repeat it. Since the teller was not ashamed to repeat the information before a group, you may assume that the positive interpretation was intended. This permission does not hold if the teller is a renowned gossip or gives a negative interpretation to the matter, as indicated either explicitly or by tone of voice or bodily expression.

"Well, everybody," said Louella, the town gossip, "Guess what! Anna's having a baby. At her age—can you imagine!"

Since Louella clearly placed a negative interpretation on the news, the others should treat it as a secret and not repeat it.

"Guess what!" said Elena, Anna's best friend, "Anna is having a baby!"

Since Elena announced the news to a group and clearly intended a positive interpretation, it is acceptable to repeat this news to others. The information does not have to be treated as a secret.

If you repeat to others information which is open to interpretation, having heard it before a group, it is important to make absolutely certain that you do not give a negative twist to the information in the way that you repeat it.

For example:

Sally says to her book group, "Elise gave a hundred dollars to the library association this week!" Later that day Beth repeats the news to some friends. She says, "Can you believe it? That wealthy Elise, who claims to be so civic-minded, gave a gift to the library association of only a hundred dollars."

It could have been acceptable for Beth to repeat the information about Elise. She heard it before a group and it was spoken in a complimentary way. But since Beth took a negative attitude to the information, she should have treated it as a secret.

PILLOW TALK

Many people who are generally good at keeping secrets tell everything they hear to their wives or husbands. They assume that "my spouse is as myself." This is not the case. *One should not repeat secrets to one's spouse.* This is no different than telling a secret to anyone else. You cannot know if the person who told you a secret would mind your spouse knowing. You cannot be sure that your spouse will not repeat the news to someone whom the original speaker would prefer does not hear it.

It is true that married people constitute a single unit in many respects. They are responsible to fulfill each other's contracts. They are spiritually one flesh and one soul. But they are still two different people for the purpose of telling and keeping secrets. One may think that everybody assumes that people tell everything they hear to their spouses. That is largely true, but when it comes to secrets it is always better to err on the side of discretion.

As a rabbi, I hear many secrets from my congregants. I do not repeat these secrets to my wife. Often a member of my congregation will begin to discuss a private matter with her.

"I'm sorry," says Cheryl, "but I do not know what you are talking about."

"Really!" says the person. "But I told your husband all about it last week. Why didn't he tell you?"

"My husband does not tell me any confidences unless people specifically give him permission to share the information with his wife. I don't tell him any confidences, either, so if you want him to know something, you cannot just tell me and count on me to pass on the information. You have to tell him yourself."

Cheryl says: *It often puts me in an embarrassing situation when people are talking about something important to them and I don't know anything about it. Sometimes it puts my husband on the spot when people tell me something in confidence and then wait for him to react.*

Still, I think it is extremely valuable that my husband and I do not exchange people's secrets. People gain confidence that when they tell the rabbi something it will not be blabbed to everyone. Also, people learn to tell him things directly instead of counting on the grapevine to get a message across. Sometimes people are embarrassed to tell something directly to the rabbi, especially if they are being critical or are afraid of being judged. It is much healthier for the congregation when people realize that they have to say things directly, and not rely on gossip to accomplish their communications."

If you think someone who is telling you a secret may intend for you to tell your spouse, you can always ask.

"Rabbi, I'm sorry to tell you that my mother has cancer."

"I'm very sorry to hear that. Do you mind if I tell my wife, so that she can drop in on her and see how she's doing?"

In this case, if I do not repeat the information to my wife, people might think that she does not care for the sick or that she is not compassionate. Even in a case like this, it is wrong to repeat the information unless you have asked. The reply to the request might be "Yes, please tell your wife," but it might also be "The family doesn't want anyone to know this right now, but thank you for asking, just the same." Unless you ask you do not know what matters should be kept secret even from your own spouse.

Just as one should not reveal secrets to one's spouse, one should not reveal secrets to any other member of the household or family.

GOING BEYOND THE RULE

It is generally acceptable to repeat information about a person heard in a group if that information is not gossip. It is a good idea not to take advantage of this permission. One should develop a reputation for not talking about others even in permissible matters. It can only redound to your credit if you are known as a person who treats all information about others as a secret.

CLOSED MEETINGS

The deliberations of closed meetings are not to be divulged. This includes meetings of government, business, social, and charitable organizations. If you attend a closed meeting, you should not repeat to anyone outside the group what subjects were raised at the meeting or who said what. You must be especially careful not to divulge how individuals voted in a closed session vote or election.

If matters affecting a person outside the meeting were discussed and voted upon, the organization will inform this person of the results of its deliberations through the proper channels, or else the subject will realize from the subsequent actions of the organization what its decision was. One must not reveal to the subject who voted in his favor and who against, except when this is a matter of public record.

Those who are present at a closed meeting have a right to speak freely and vote their conscience without having their words or their votes revealed.

If there is some question as to whether a particular meeting is open or private, you may inquire. It may be necessary to inspect the charter or bylaws of the organization in question to see whether the meeting should be open or closed. The leaders of the meeting may desire to have a closed meeting, but if the bylaws of the organization require an open meeting, it is permissible to divulge to others what was said and how people voted.

The votes of elected government officials are a matter of public record and are open to praise or criticism in the interest of an informed citizenry.

REVEALING SECRETS TO ADVISORS

It is permissible to reveal secrets to professional advice givers, such as psychiatrists, psychologists, lawyers, and marriage counselors. Professional advisors take no personal interest in hearing your secrets, and will not use them to make judgments about the people involved. They listen only for the sake of rendering assistance to you. The professional advice giver is duty bound to maintain the privacy of all your communications and to give no indication to others through word or deed as to what you might have said about them.

The paid professional advisor is, in a sense, an extension of your own self. Sharing a secret with an advisor might be necessary to help you work through a problem. If the problem involves your feelings toward another person, sharing your secrets and dealing with them in a professional setting might even help you to refrain from improper gossip.

If you discover that your paid advisor is not keeping your secrets, find another advisor. Report the violation of your confidence to the advisor's employer or to the appropriate professional governing body for disciplinary action.

If you believe that your paid advisor is taking a personal interest in hearing your secrets beyond professional necessity, raise this issue with your advisor or find an advisor whose attitude strikes you as more disinterested and professional.

It is permissible to reveal secrets to a member of the clergy. Speaking to your spiritual leader is equivalent to a private confession before God. Your spiritual leader will maintain your confidence and assist you to advance from your concerns to proper action according to the dictates of your religion. He or she should not reveal your confidences to others nor pass judgment on others based on your words.

Be sure to exercise great caution in sharing secrets with casual advisors—friends with whom you share your thoughts because you trust their insight and value their advice. You must consider whether the people you discuss with your friendly advisor would want their secrets known to this person. Remember that a friendly advisor has no professional obligation to be discreet. Also, be careful that you are not using advice-seeking as an excuse to gossip to a friend.

Beware of statements like the following:

"Louise, you are so good with people! Please tell me what I should do about so-and-so because she is doing such-and-such which annoys me, and nothing I do seems to stop her."

Is this really a request for advice, or just an excuse for gossip? Before sharing this matter with your friendly advisor, be certain that your only desire is to receive wise advice on how to handle the situation. Then be sure to reveal only the necessary facts, without exaggeration and without using judgmental language. Make it clear to your friend that you only wish to hear practical advice, and you will not listen to words that judge the person whose actions are troubling you. Be certain in advance that you really intend to follow the advice of your wise friend. If not, there is no good reason to share this secret. Use as a friendly advisor only someone who will maintain your confidence and not repeat your confessions before others as gossip.

Chapter 8
Confession

THE POWER OF THE TONGUE

Up to this point we have discussed the harm that can come from the misuse of words. In chapters 8 and 9 we will consider speech that is recommended because it has the power to do good—to reverse harm, to right wrongs, to relieve suffering. The tongue, which can cause so much suffering through gossip, has an equal power to bring good into the world. Words can hurt more than sticks and stones, or words can bring healing, sometimes more than the most powerful medicines. Silence is golden, but there is infinite value in knowing when to say a good word.

CONFESSION IN RELIGION AND IN HUMAN RELATIONS

Confession of sin plays a significant role in Judaism, Christianity, and Islam. These religions affirm the absolute and infinite power of confession to make us right with God. The message of repentance is equally wise and valid in the earthly realm of human relations. Whatever works to bring us back into God's grace works equally well to bring us back into the favor of our fellow human beings. As confession has the power to remove all sin from us and make us pure before God, so also does confession to a fellow human being remove all anger, hatred, and desire for retribution, making us beloved of men and women.

We learn from religious tradition that no one is ever so far gone as to be beyond repentance. Even repentance with one's dying breath after a lifetime of evil deeds, if sincere, is wholly acceptable before God. In the same way, no matter how much we have wronged others, if we confess and humble ourselves we will eventually be able to win our way back into their good graces. Perhaps we have wronged a person in such a way that we are unable to undo what we have done on a material level. Perhaps we have destroyed something irreplaceable. Maybe we have robbed someone of a special moment that will never return. We may have engaged in gossip and spread a rumor that cannot be called back. Do not think that because the wrong cannot be undone one can never return to grace. Confession has the power to win complete forgiveness.

The *Rubaiyat of Omar Khayyam* says: "The Moving Finger writes; and, having writ, Moves on: nor all your Piety nor Wit Shall lure it back to cancel half a Line, Nor all your Tears wash out a Word of it." This is not quite true. Confession can rewrite the past, making what is as if it were not, what happened as if it never happened.

We are taught that one who confesses stands on a higher spiritual level than one who has never sinned. "The penitent stands where even angels cannot stand" (Berakhot 34b), it is said. In the end, those who humble themselves and confess when they have wronged others will be even more beloved than before. The wrongs that were held against them will now be remembered to their credit.

If by some chance you have never done anything wrong in your whole life and have never been mistaken about anything, then you are stuck on a very low spiritual rung. To rise to a higher level, be wrong for once, and then confess!

Bear in mind, however, that if you say, "I will do wrong and then confess, and thus get away with it," your confession will not accomplish what you intend. Repentance must be utterly sincere. An apology is only valid if it is accompanied by sincere regret. The one thing that cannot be faked is sincerity.

THE POWER OF CONFESSION

I first learned the power of confession from my friend Rob Schwarz, who is now an Episcopal priest. At the time, he and I were seniors in high school.

Rob and I cut a class one day and went to the library to talk. Suddenly we saw Mr. F____, the librarian, coming straight toward us. We knew that he was going to ask to see our library passes, and then we would be caught. The penalty for cutting class was a three-day suspension from school. Mr. F____ lifted a finger ominously and opened his mouth, but before he could utter a sound Rob blurted out these words: "I'm sorry we were talking, Mr. F____. We'll be quiet now and get right down to work."

"Oh, all right," said Mr. F____. He went back to his desk.

We studied quietly until the bell rang and we could leave the library, safe from all charges. "That was brilliant!" I said to Rob. "How did you know that it would work?"

"Simple!" said Rob. "Once you've confessed to someone, he can't do a thing to you. He loses the heart to punish you."

Nobody can punish you once you have confessed. There is so much power in this simple truism. It pays never to forget this lesson. What a deal! Every action has a consequence, but you can get away without paying for your misdeeds if you will just confess. Even those convicted of serious crimes get a lighter sentence if they confess and express regret for their misdeeds. Confession is such a powerful weapon in the arsenal of simple tricks for succeeding in life, it is a wonder that the message eludes so many people, who never seem to take advantage of this amazing offer.

There are some good reasons that people do not confess even when they have so much to gain. Let us examine these reasons and try to overcome them in ourselves.

IMPEDIMENTS TO CONFESSION

Confession is a display of humility and mortal weakness. We often find it very difficult to put ourselves into an "inferior" position before another person. When we confess we put someone else above ourselves. The person to whom we confess has the power either to be gracious and grant us pardon or to be vindictive and refuse to forgive. Either way we risk humiliation when we confess.

When we feel humiliated we may imagine that we have earned the contempt of others. Many people feel that by confession they will lose their dignity and honor.

When we know we should confess, it is because we know we have done something wrong. We are on the defensive. Our deeply ingrained, primitive instincts take over when we are feeling defensive. Our instincts tell us to fight for our lives, to fight savagely. When we are on the defensive it seems as if life itself is at stake and we have everything to lose.

Instead of surviving through surrender, we engage in a fierce verbal battle. We deny having done anything wrong. We justify our actions and defend them, no matter how absurd. We counterattack by blaming the victim of our wrongdoing for somehow causing or encouraging it. We do anything but accept blame.

In an earlier chapter we discussed the tendency to attribute the best possible motives to our actions. We can always find a million good reasons for everything we do. But it is just plain difficult to open our eyes and see clearly that we have wronged another person. Until we can admit to doing wrong we will not be able to confess and win pardon.

THE BENEFIT OF CONFESSION

Consider the case of another social creature, the dog. In every pack of dogs there is a social order. The higher dogs lord it over the lower dogs. If two dogs get into a disagreement they fight it out to see which is top dog. The losing dog risks severe injury or even death, but he has an out. If he rolls over and bares his neck, in a posture of utter helplessness, the other dog is unable to attack him further. The fight is over. Which dog got the best of the deal? The winner got to be top dog. The loser tangled with a more powerful dog and came away with his life. The "loser" gained more than the "winner." That is the power of confession. You confess when you realize that you were wrong and another person was right. By confessing you put yourself in someone else's power, but you gain more than the other person does. If you refuse to confess and it is revealed that you are in the wrong, then you are in the position of the lower dog who refuses to roll over. He has gained nothing and lost everything.

The wise person will come to see that it is foolish to avoid confession. Why refuse to confess when there is so much to be gained? It is more than worth our while to train ourselves to overcome those instincts that prevent us from confessing. Confession is so beneficial to us that we ought to confess to gain the love and approval of others even when we know in our hearts that we are right and they are wrong. If we are so perfect that we never do anything wrong, we ought to do something wrong on purpose every now and then just so that we will have an excuse to endear ourselves to others through confession.

Bill got into an argument with his wife, Heather, over which was a better baseball team, the Mets or the Yankees. Bill spent a lot of time studying baseball statistics and watching games, while Heather was at best a casual baseball fan. Bill was certain in his heart that he was right. Nevertheless, he knew that his relationship with Heather was more important than winning a pointless battle. That evening at dinner, Bill said to Heather, "I was wrong to argue with you about baseball teams. You were right about the Yankees and Mets. I'm sorry."

Heather said to Bill, "Oh, Bill, no wonder I love you. You're a great guy!"

The secret to confession is this: We always rise in the esteem of those who receive our confession. The fear of humiliation exists only in our imagination. Take a moment to think about the people who have confessed to you. They are very likely the people you love and admire the most. Why? Because by confessing to you they made you feel good about yourself, and what more could we ask from another person?

When I was in the second grade I had a disagreement with my teacher over the name of the author of a certain book. The next day I got the book and showed it to my teacher, Miss Wagner. She said to me, "I apologize. I can see that you were right and I was wrong."

I remember three things about this incident. First, I remember the shock of realizing that a teacher, the highest authority figure in my life experience, could be wrong. To a young child, it is a revelation to realize that a teacher is fallible. This was a valuable lesson for a child to learn. If a teacher can be wrong sometimes then anyone can—and that is a good lesson for life, because it is true.

Second, I remember how good the whole incident made me feel about myself. I must be real smart, I thought, if I could teach a teacher something.

Third, I remember how high Miss Wagner rose in my esteem on account of her confession. It made her seem more God-like, more wonderful than ever in my eyes. I had feared that she would be angry at me for showing her up, but she was so gracious! To this day I remember Miss Wagner with the greatest affection, in large part on account of that incident.

What I experienced with my teacher was a universal human experience. The people we love and admire most are those who do not stand on their dignity but confess when they are wrong.

This is a particularly valuable lesson for leaders. All leaders must make many decisions. Inevitably they will make some errors of judgment. It is too easy to stick to a futile idea or an unpopular course of action just because one's ego is invested in it. When this happens, one can save endless aggravation, and possibly one's job or leadership position, by the simple expedient of confession. It is never too late to say: "I've been doing this wrong. I should have followed Fran's plan in the first place. Let's start doing it her way." Not only will you accomplish more, but you will seem like much more of a leader and gain the admiration of your group.

FORGIVENESS

We should be quick to forgive. When someone has confessed to wronging you, it is proper to forgive that person immediately. If you hold a grudge and refuse to accept an apology, you now bear the burden of the original wrong on your own head.

Everyone ought to be quick to forgive, but if we confess to another person who is not forgiving, we must be prepared to apologize again and again until our apology is accepted.

If someone humbles himself before you, confessing and asking forgiveness, do not make him grovel and purchase your forgiveness with self-humiliation, or else when you do finally forgive you will not receive credit for graciousness. Forget about revenge and be quick to forgive.

I told my friend Rob how he taught me the meaning of repentance in the high school library. He did not remember the incident. "You taught me the meaning of repentance," he said, "during our freshman year of college."

"I did?" I said. "When? How?"

"I wronged you in some way, and you were so angry with me that you cut off our friendship. I cornered you and apologized to you. You started yelling and screaming at me. 'Darn you!' you

said. 'I don't want to be your friend anymore, but now I have to be, because you apologized, and my religion commands me to forgive you. !@#$%& you!' That's when I learned that you have to forgive someone who repents. It's not a matter of choice."

I have no memory of this incident, but I'm proud to have taught the meaning of repentance to the person who taught me the meaning of repentance. It is true. If you are a person of faith, you have no choice but to forgive.

According to Jewish law, if someone refuses to accept your apology, you must come back again with two witnesses and apologize in front of them. If the person still does not accept your apology, you may interrupt the worship service on the Sabbath to confess and apologize before the entire congregation. Who could be so hard-hearted as to refuse to accept such an apology? Who would shame himself before the congregation by refusing to forgive?

If someone confesses to you and begs your forgiveness, it is absolutely wrong to say, "Oh, you didn't do anything, really. There's no need to apologize." That is really just another way of saying "I refuse to forgive you!" Someone who chooses to apologize to you has a need to apologize, whether or not you think so. The only ethical thing to do is to graciously accept the apology. Refusing to acknowledge that a wrong has been committed is a lowly way of refusing to be a gracious and forgiving person.

HOW TO REPENT

To seek forgiveness from God or from another person we engage in the process that religion calls "repentance." The Hebrew term is *teshuva*, which means "turning." There are three stages to repentance.

The first stage is to admit that you have done wrong. The second is to regret the wrong that you have done. The third is a decision never to repeat this wrong. A true apology requires all three stages. For example:

"John, I took more than my share of the profits from our joint venture. I am overwhelmed with sorrow for the way I cheated you. I will repay all that I owe you out of our future profits, and never cheat you again."

"Sally, I admit that I went out with Rita. I should not have done that when we were going steady. I am sorry that I betrayed your trust, and it now pains me to think of how I hurt you. I will be totally honest with you in the future."

"Jan, the truth is I just forgot that it was your birthday. It was so thoughtless of me! I want to take you to dinner tonight along with some of our friends for a late celebration. Let's make tonight everything your birthday ought to be!"

The first stage is confession. The best way to do this is to state explicitly what it is that you did wrong. If you do not think that you did wrong but are apologizing for the effect of your actions, then you should confess to that effect.

"Jack, I hurt your feelings when I went fishing without you."

"Heather, I made you very angry by ignoring your advice."

One could confess and yet feel no regret.

"Yes I told everybody what you did to me, and I hope you suffer what I suffered from you."

"Sure I killed him, and if I could bring him back to life, I would kill him again."

The second stage of repentance is to express sincere regret for what you have done. The magic words are: *"I'm sorry!"*

The third stage of repentance is to express your resolve that you have learned your lesson. As far as you are concerned, you never intend to commit this wrong again. If you are fortunate, you may fall into a situation of temptation where you will have a chance to prove your resolve. Even if your resolve is only theoretical, because a similar situation will never again arise, it is still important to grow personally past the weakness that let you go astray and wrong another person.

If you can undo the wrong you have done, you should make that a part of your repentance. If the wrong cannot be undone, your confession, regret, and resolve will be sufficient if they are sincere. The person you wronged ought then to be convinced that you are a changed person and will not find it too difficult to forgive you.

REPENTANCE FOR GOSSIPING

A person came to his rabbi and said to him, "Rabbi, I have gossiped against all the people in town. Now I regret what I have done. Please assign me a penance." The rabbi plucked a dandelion and blew on it, so that the white seeds flew off into the air. "Your penance is to gather all the dandelion seeds and bring them back to me," said the rabbi. "How can I do that?" cried the man, "the seeds have scattered to the four winds!" "Well," said the rabbi, "so has your gossip. Nevertheless, confess before God, be ashamed, and resolve never to gossip again, and you will be forgiven!"

If you have been guilty of listening to gossip, you must do the following: Resolve in your mind that you will not believe the gossip you have heard. Review in your mind the gossip you have listened to, and tell yourself concerning each instance that the speaker must have been mistaken, or else there were mitigating circumstances about which you know nothing. Be sure that the next time you see the subject of the gossip you do not remember or in any way act upon the bad things you heard.

Follow the three stages of repentance outlined above. Confess in your heart that you have been guilty of listening to gossip. Feel regret for participating in gossip. Resolve not to repeat the same error in the future. Consider the concrete steps that you will take in order to avoid falling into the pattern of gossip. Review the guidelines set forth in this book.

If you are a religious person, pray to God to strengthen you against the sin of gossiping. That is a prayer that will surely be heard. God will assist you in whatever you resolve. If you resolve to be a gossip, you will find help to become a biting and witty gossip. If you resolve to refrain from gossip, God will help you to strengthen your will so that you will be able to refuse to speak or listen to gossip.

If you have gossiped, go to those you gossiped to and retract what you said. Say to them, "You know what I said to you about so-and-so? Well, on second thought I take it back. I was wrong to speak that way, and I think I may have been mistaken in my judgment. I may have gotten the facts mixed up. Please forgive me for speaking falsehood to you!" If you are quick you may be able to retract what you said before it is repeated to anyone else. If you succeed in taking back your improper statements before they are repeated, you need not confess the wrong to the person about whom you gossiped.

By the time you regret your action the gossip may have spread beyond hope of recovery. If that is the case, confess to the person you wronged and ask forgiveness. You do not have to specify exactly what you said, since this may be too embarrassing and may increase the hard feelings between you. It is sufficient to admit spreading gossip and request forgiveness. Offer your complete cooperation in undoing any damage you may have done to your victim.

Chapter 9
Words of Comfort and Consolation

Pleasant words are like a honeycomb, sweet to the palate and a cure for the body.
—Proverbs 16:24

VISITING THE SICK

The Talmud tells the following story:

Rabbi Akiva once noticed that one of his disciples had been absent from school for several days. "Where is he?" Rabbi Akiva asked the other students. "We do not know," they replied. Rabbi Akiva went to the student's home and found him alone and unattended, sick in bed. Rabbi Akiva cared for him and visited with him. The student regained his health. When he returned to school he said to Rabbi Akiva, "If you had not come to visit me, I would not have recovered." After that Rabbi Akiva used to say: "Whoever does not visit the sick is guilty of murder" (Nedarim 40a).

One should be sure to visit the hospital or bedside whenever a family member, friend, or acquaintance is laid up by an illness or accident. Your visit might mean the difference between death and recovery. Caring human contact is the most powerful medicine known. All of our modern wonder drugs and high-technology treatments have not replaced the need for human warmth. If anything, they have increased that need. The patient in the modern hospital comes to feel like a helpless cog in a wellness machine. The patient feels a great need for someone to enter the room, not to perform a procedure, but just to relate as one human being to another.

Some people are in the hospital to get better. Others go into the hospital to die. In either case friendly contact with caring visitors is essential to treatment. Even if one is to die shortly, one is still a part of this world as long as one is alive. In the final hours of life the need for meaningful contact with other people is stronger than ever.

All too often we do not visit the sick, even though we know that we should. One thing that keeps us from our doing duty is the fear that we do not know what to say.

FEAR OF TALKING TO THE SICK

As a student rabbi I found visiting the sick to be my most difficult duty. I never knew what to say. One night I went to dinner with two cousins, a hospital social worker and a medical doctor whose specialty brought him into contact with many dying teenagers. I told my cousins, Anne Tarrow and Bob Blum, about my difficulty in visiting hospital patients. I asked them to tell me some great things to say, from their own experience, that would make visiting the sick easy and pleasant.

I did not yet know that there are no such magic words. But Bob, the doctor, taught me something more valuable than the "right" thing to say. He told me about a sixteen-year-old patient of his. She was dying in the hospital, and her school friends did not come to visit her. She understood why; they stayed away because they did not know what to say. This girl said to Bob, "Don't they know, it doesn't matter what people say? If they want to be here with me, I will know it."

It does not matter what you say, as long as you want to be there.

That is the whole secret. The reason we often do not know what to say is that there is no right thing to say. That is not what matters. No matter what you say, the mere fact that you come to visit says all that needs to be said. Your words during your visit, or lack of words, just fill in the space of time.

There actually are many "wrong" things that you could say in a hospital visit. These include wishing a quick recovery to a patient whose illness is terminal and telling a patient in pain and despair how wonderful life is. Or you might bring up a subject intended to distract that instead increases the patient's feeling of pain. You might say something that will arouse your friend's fear of death and suffering. A hospital room is a minefield of possible misstatements. But in the end, none of this matters. After you have left the sickroom, what you said will soon be forgotten. Whether you were entertaining, cheering and comforting, or tongue-tied and awkward, by the next day it will not be remembered. Your friend will only remember that you cared enough to overcome your discomfort and be there. If you should return for a second visit, that will be remembered to your greater credit.

WHAT TO SAY IN THE PRESENCE OF THE SICK

Even though it does not matter what you say, there are some guidelines that can make your visit to the sick as pleasant and comforting as possible.

Discuss with the sick the same things that interest them when they are well. If they love television, talk about television shows. If they love sports, discuss sports. If they are involved in home and family life, discuss their children's activities. People do not change inwardly just because they are sick. You may think, "He'll be dead in a week. What does it matter how the Phillies are doing?" If he was a Phillies fan all his life, he will be a Phillies fan also in the last week of life. (Maybe more so; as they say, "misery loves company.")

It is difficult to know whether or not to ask sick people about the state of their health. Some want to talk about it, others want to avoid it at all costs. Most doctors nowadays believe in full disclosure of a patient's condition, but not all agree. In any event, this refers only to the doctor-patient relationship and not to friendly visits. It is not your obligation to discuss with the patient every detail of her condition, unless that is her wish.

We do not want to hem in the dying with a wall of silence by avoiding the topic of death. On the other hand, we do not want to force them to discuss something they find terrifying. The best thing is to be sufficiently open that a patient who wishes to raise the subject of death can do so. Without ever speaking of death you can have an open demeanor that lets it be known that you will not be frightened away by any topic the patient may choose to raise.

Do not claim to have answers for life's unanswerable questions. Nobody knows why God grants long life to some, few years and suffering to others. It is not your task to defend God or justify horrible events. Rather than give a pat response to the question "Why?", join your friend in tears. Do not be afraid to cry!

It is always appropriate to pray. One prayer you might say is the following:

Our God and God of all ages, heal us and we shall be healed, save us and we shall be saved, for we place our hope in You. Grant perfect healing to ____, health of body and peace of mind, along with all others who are in need of Your healing power, for You are a great and powerful Ruler who is faithful to heal. Blessed are You, O God, who heals the sick.

Prayer should not be a shield behind which we hide, but a way of reaching out for hope and of expressing concern. You could always ask the patient before praying, "Is there anything in particular that you would like me to include in my prayer?" This is a wonderful opening to hearing the patient's concerns.

A visit to the sick can be nerve-racking. Sometimes we are tempted to make foolish statements just to relieve the tension. Think twice before saying things like the following:

"I'm sure that you'll be better in no time."

"Everything that God does is for the best, even if we can't see it clearly now."

"You look wonderful!"

Are these statements really appropriate to the situation, or are you just saying them because you find it unbearable to be in the presence of so much suffering and sorrow?

Never say, "I know just what you are feeling." Though well-meant, this can sound as if you are making light of the sufferings of your friend. If you have suffered through a similar trauma, relating your own experience and how you survived it can be extremely helpful. There is nothing like a support group! The best-trained professional counselors are never so helpful as the sharing of experience. Many people have turned their suffering into a high and spiritual service by lending emotional support to those who come after them into a similar situation.

If you made some errors in what you said when visiting a sick friend, do not fret about it. Do not punish yourself. Do not let it stop you from visiting again. You were there, and that is the important thing. Whatever you said, it was words spoken lovingly by one human being to another. On your next visit do not waste time apologizing, but just try again to be the most caring friend you can be.

CONSOLING MOURNERS

It is important to visit mourners and console them for the loss of their loved ones. The proper time for a consolation visit varies according to the religious and ethnic tradition of the mourners. Find out what is appropriate for the people you are consoling and visit them at that time. In Jewish tradition the proper time for a visit is during the week following the burial, particularly later on the day of the funeral. Every organized religion provides a formal setting for consolers to greet mourners and express their sympathies. The formal ritual of mourning, when it is known to mourners and consolers, is extremely helpful in allowing grief to run its course. Mourners with no religious tradition can be at a disadvantage in not having a social system for receiving consolation and dealing with loss.

Many people avoid making consolation calls for the same reason that they avoid visiting the sick in the hospital. They do not know what to say. We repeat here what we said about visiting the sick. It does not matter what you say, as long as you want to be there.

WHAT TO SAY TO MOURNERS

It is so easy to get tongue-tied while trying to convey our sorrow and sympathy to a mourner. The solution is that one should not try to say it all. Don't worry! The mourners will understand what you feel and what you are trying to say. They are as human as you. Understatement is best in expressing sorrow. To go on and on implies that you really could sum up all of the grief that the mourners feel and all of the goodness of the deceased. To speak briefly implies a better message, that the depth of true grief is beyond words. The best thing to say on a consolation call is the following: "I am sorry for your loss. May God console you."

If you spend some time with the mourners, there will be opportunity for reflective conversation in which you can express your thoughts and feelings. The best advice is to let the mourners choose the topic of conversation and follow their lead. They may have moments when they wish to talk about the deceased, and other moments when they need to distract themselves with light conversation. Everyone grieves in their own way and no topic is inappropriate.

As with visiting the sick, your presence is more important than the content of your conversation.

As I was working on this chapter I shared in a tragedy with a family in my congregation. They and their guests were gathered in the temple to celebrate a bar mitzvah, and while the party was in progress the boy's grandfather died in his home city a few hours' drive away. The boy's parents and grandmother were brought to the temple office, full of fresh grief but not wanting to discomfit their guests. I went in to be with them and stood by the side of the new widow, feeling like a fool for not having anything to say. I stood with the family in excruciating silence for an hour or two, until the party ended. All this time I wanted to flee, to hide my own feeling of failure for having nothing to say. I stayed because I wanted to be a comforting friend. And, since I was writing this chapter at the time, I knew I should practice what I preach. The next day the family asked me to conduct the funeral. They explained that the widow had asked for me, even though there were many rabbis in her home city, because "I had been so comforting at the time of death." Apparently I was not as much of a fool as I'd felt at the time. Being there was what counted.

WHAT NOT TO SAY TO MOURNERS

Your role as a consoler is to provide the support that will allow the mourners to feel free to sink into the depths of grief, from which they can eventually arise renewed for life.

Do not say anything which will stop the free flow of grief. Above all, say nothing to indicate that you do not want any strong expressions of emotion to take place in your presence.

Do not say to mourners: "Be strong! Don't cry! Everything will be all right!"

When you tell mourners to be strong, you are telling them to be strong for you, so that you do not have to deal with their grief and pain. But you have come to help them with their grief and pain. You must be strong, so that they can be weak.

Do not say to mourners, "There, there, everything will be all right." This may very well not be the case. When children are orphaned, or parents have lost a child, life will never be the same for them. Things will not be all right. At this time of grief, express your sorrow. Later, when the first stages of mourning are concluded, express your hope for a brighter future.

There are different opinions about the value of discussing with mourners the hope for heavenly reward or the belief that death is a benefit from God. The decision to raise this topic must be based entirely on the mourners' belief system (and not on your own beliefs). Those who deeply hold such beliefs will be comforted by the mention of them. Those who do not will be outraged to hear them in their hour of grief. You may encourage the faith of the mourners, but do not attempt to convert them to your faith, even if you feel in your heart that it would provide them with a valuable consolation. Do not say that the deceased has been called home to God unless you are sure that the mourners also feel this way.

Do not tell mourners that you understand their grief. You may honestly feel that you do, but in their hour of grief most people feel that no one has ever suffered as they are suffering. Rather than say that you understand what they are feeling, it is better to tell mourners that you are sure that their grief is beyond comprehension. You may wish to share with the mourners your own experience of grief and recovery, especially if your loss was similar to what they are now experiencing. As with visiting the sick, there is much help in sharing with a support group.

Help the mourners to talk out their grief by asking direct or indirect questions about the deceased. For example:

"Tell me about your mother."

"What do you miss about your father the most?"

"What things will change for you now?"

If the mourners do not wish to discuss the deceased, do not force the issue. They may appreciate a repeat opportunity at another time.

Criticizing mourners when they have completed the mourning process and are ready to go on with their lives is a source of much malicious gossip.

"Look at her, dancing on his grave! Less than a year after her husband's death, and she's going out on a date. Doesn't she have any feelings?"

Life must go on. It is proper for those who have lost a spouse to date and remarry after a period of mourning has passed. It is a compliment to a deceased spouse if the survivor wishes to reenter married life.

All friends and relatives are expected to make at least one consolation call after a death. This is no less than an absolute duty. If you make a return visit, this will be perceived as an act of pure love and grace on your part. A good time to make an extra consolation call is shortly after the official mourning period has ended. This is a difficult time of transition. A friendly follow-up visit is especially welcome at this time.

CONSOLING THOSE WHO HAVE SUFFERED AN EMBARRASSING LOSS

It is difficult to speak to a patient in a hospital or to a person who is grieving. It is even more difficult to speak to a person who has just suffered an embarrassing loss. This category includes recent separation or divorce, bankruptcy, conviction of a crime, loss of a romance, failure to be accepted to a college, loss of a job, and many other similar things.

It is hard to be with sick and grieving people. Their presence reminds us too much of our own mortality. It is even more difficult to be with people suffering from a personal loss. Their embarrassment embarrasses us. There is an element of blame, since every such loss is at least theoretically avoidable.

There is another good reason that it is hard to be with people who have suffered an embarrassing loss. In response to their suffering, they are likely to be unpleasant in their speech and actions. It is only in the movies that suffering ennobles the sufferer. In real life suffering diminishes, making the victim obnoxious, boring, and boorish. No wonder that "nobody loves you when you're down and out." One is not very lovable at times like these.

It is an especially good deed to reach out in friendship to those who have suffered embarrassing losses. In order to do this, you must overlook their angry, aggressive, or defensive statements. You must not lose patience while someone in this situation tells a tale of woe over and over again. You must tolerate expressions of bitterness and anger, and complaints about how unfair life is.

Often we will say things like this about a friend in a time of loss:

"I would like to be friends with her, but she keeps driving me away."

"I would spend more time with him if he didn't insist on telling about his rotten boss over and over again."

"He's so angry all the time. How can he expect any sympathy?"

Those who expect their suffering friends to be humble and appreciative, so that it is easy to be nice to them, need a new concept of what it means to be a true friend to a person in a time of need. Anyone can be kind, friendly, and sympathetic to a person who is in a stable emotional condition. It is precisely because your friend in this time of loss is so obnoxious and unbearable that your words of kindness and consolation are sorely needed. Your reward will come much later. For now, your noble virtue is to be patient and gentle while your friend, who needs you so badly, does everything possible to push you away.

Jeff has recently suffered a loss of self-esteem through a variety of setbacks, losing his job and being a subject of common gossip over some foolish things he did. Jeff's friend Bert stops by to express his support.

"Get the heck out of here, Bert!" said Jeff. "I don't need you and I don't need your sympathy! I'll be fine!"

"You can say what you want, Jeff," said Bert, "But I refuse to stop being your friend. I'm going to sit right here with you and keep on being your friend no matter what you say to me!"

"Darn, but you're a stubborn jerk," said Jeff. "OK, then, since you leave me no choice, let's go down to the diner and have a cup of coffee."

Bert knows how to be a real friend.

This is what people who are suffering an embarrassing loss hear over and over again: "We're so sorry to hear of your troubles. We must have you over for dinner sometime soon. Well, we must be running along now. Good luck!" Needless to say, the dinner invitation never comes. This constant distancing and rejection from old friends can be more painful and embarrassing than the original loss. At the very hour when one most needs a human touch and a friendly gesture, one is locked into a vicious cycle of loneliness, because no one wants to be with a person who is going through such hard times.

A personal loss may cause grief surprisingly similar to that caused by illness and death. To lose a spouse through divorce, for example, can feel the same as being widowed. As with the response to other causes of grief, your loving presence is more important than what you say. Engage in friendly chatter. Try to distract your friend from thinking about her troubles. Get your friend involved in the real-life concerns of other people. This will decrease your friend's self-absorption and make her a more attractive person to be with. If a friend wishes to discuss his or her troubles, lend a sympathetic ear, but do not encourage self-pity.

Do not chastise your friend or tell him what he could have done to avoid his troubles. As much as possible, act as you did when things were going well. Help your friend to discover the truth that no matter what may happen, he is still the same person on the inside.

"Cal, I'm so sorry to hear that you lost your job! I know that being district manager meant the world to you. Look, please come for dinner Tuesday night at 6:00. I know that Joan and the kids will be so glad to see you, as they always are. No, don't bring the wine; I think you should conserve your financial resources right now, but I'll let you buy me a bottle of good wine when you get your next job. I tell you what—would you mind if I also invited another friend who knows some people in business? He might be able to help you expand your network for your job search—and if not, he's someone you'll enjoy meeting anyway. No, no excuses—be there! Great!"

CONCLUSION

If you master the art of giving consolation, you will transform your tongue into an instrument of life, healing, and goodness. There is no trick, no words so clever and on target that they will always provide comfort. The real trick is to care about people. The words will follow.

Chapter 10
Summation

> A knowledgeable person is sparing with words, a person of understanding is reticent. Even a fool, if he keeps silent, is deemed wise, intelligent, if he seals his lips.
>
> —Proverbs 17:27–28

> The tongue is like an arrow. If a person raises a sword to kill his fellow and then changes his mind, he can return the sword to its scabbard. But the arrow, once it has been fired, cannot be called back.
>
> —Midrash Sohar Tov 120

MAKE A GOOD TRADE

Every transaction takes place on two levels. On the material level, goods and money are exchanged, with each party attempting to maximize profit or gain. On the psychic level, each party to a transaction wants to come out with increased self-esteem. We want to complete a transaction feeling like winners, feeling good about ourselves.

You can help the other party in any transaction to grow in self-esteem. You have a currency at your disposal more valuable than all of the goods or services you can offer. This currency is kind words of praise. You can actually use this currency in place of hard cash. Most people will sell at a lower price or buy at a higher price for the privilege of doing business with a person who makes them feel good about themselves.

The wise make good use of the currency of a good word. Sadly, many people see deal-making as a war with a winner and a loser, rather than as an agreement in which both sides come out ahead. They wish to defeat their opponent on both levels, the material and the psychic. They want to buy low, sell high, and then make the other person feel like a fool for selling low and buying high.

The most sensible course is to take a profit in one category and give it in the other. If you want to purchase self-esteem, give away your goods for a song. If you want to make a good bargain on the material level, be ready to grant praise and trade away bragging rights. Let your transaction partner feel like a generous person and a good deal-maker.

When someone gives you a good price, do not go around saying, "Boy, I really got the better of him!" Instead, say, "He is so generous, and he knows how to please a customer. He really gave me a good deal!" When this person hears that you speak well of him, he will want to deal kindly with you again in the future. You have both gained.

Some transaction partners want to believe that they have gotten the better of you. They may want to win both deals, the material and the psychic. In dealing with such people, it is to your benefit not to enter the psychic contest. Let the other party think he has gotten the better of you, even if he tells people that you are a gullible fool. Let him win his war, and he will give you whatever you need from him—and if not, what is there to fight about anyway? You cannot be hurt by what this person says.

We often find ourselves at the mercy of unknown salespersons or repair persons. Judge such individuals to be righteous! Give them the benefit of the doubt! What do you have to gain by being defensive? You may as well proceed on the presumption that the salesperson or repair person is honest and wants to give you good service at a fair price.

A service provider who intends to cheat you is in a position to do so. You cannot prevent it. But by judging such individuals to be righteous you appeal to their good side. You maximize the chance that the service provider will want to give you a good deal. This person is doing something for you that you cannot do for yourself. In return you can give him or her the opportunity to experience your trust and gratitude.

THREE EASY ANSWERS

Most answers to problems of human relations are not as useful as we would want them to be. There is always some aspect to the answer that cannot be applied without art, experience, or sensitivity. That is why there is no little book with all the answers to life's problems. Some things we just have to figure out for ourselves.

You go to a workshop to learn how to catch tigers. The workshop leader tells you, "Buy a cage, get a tiger to love you, then invite it to go into the cage."

"How do you get the tiger to love you?" you ask.

"Ah," says the workshop leader, "That's the hard part."

An easy answer is an answer that always works. It requires no sensitivity or special skill. All you have to do is learn the rule, and it always applies. The same technique works in every situation, regardless of the personalities of the people involved. There are very few easy answers. Here are three that can help you a lot in your relations with other people.

Easy answer number one: *Anytime you want to say something but feel that you probably should not say it, do not say it.*

When this happens, it is always the voice of wisdom telling you to keep quiet. That other inner voice which is telling you to speak up anyway is the voice of selfishness, vengeance, and shortsightedness. If you listen to it, you will be sorry later. Give in to your good impulse. Later on, when you have time to think it over, you will realize that you saved yourself some trouble and maybe saved a friendship by remaining silent.

Easy answer number two: *Anytime you feel that you really should speak to someone, speak.*

You may be thinking about someone you know. Perhaps this person is going through some troubles. You may be saying to yourself, "I wonder if I should say something." Then you think of many reasons that you should not speak up. Maybe he doesn't want to be reminded of his loss. Maybe she wants to be left alone to grieve. Maybe you would say the wrong thing and make her feel worse.

The inner voice telling you that you ought to say something is the voice of love and compassion. That other voice which comes up with reasons to avoid the situation has its source not in reason but in the selfish part of your character. No one really wants to take on another person's problems. They remind us too much of our own mortal weakness. Overcome self-doubt and let compassion be your guide. Be a true friend and say something.

Easy answer number three: *Anytime someone asks you a personal question on a matter that you would rather not discuss, the proper answer is, "Why do you ask?"* As long as your inquisitor keeps asking questions, respond with another question.

This response is useful when someone is trying to make you reveal a secret. It is useful when a missionary challenges your religious beliefs without being asked to do so. It is useful when you decline an invitation to participate in an improper act and you are asked, "Why not?"

In the case of a secret:

"Please tell me what Arlene said about me!"

"Why do you ask?"

"Well, I just want to know, that's all."

"Why do you want to know?"

"Well, doesn't everybody want to know what others are saying about them?"

"Why would you want to know what others are saying about you?"

In the case of an uninvited missionary:

"How interesting that you are Jewish. What do you believe in as a Jew?"

"Why do you ask?"

"Well, I'm just curious, that's all."

"Why are you curious about my religious beliefs?"

"Well, I just think it's very interesting, that's all."

"Why do you think my religion is so interesting? Are you planning to become one of us?"

"No! Actually, I thought you might want to learn more about my religion."

"Thank you very much, but I am content as I am."

It is unlikely that a real missionary would break so easily in this game. A real missionary would play cat-and-mouse for a long time before admitting his or her true intention, which is not to learn more about you but to convince you of the truth of his or her own faith.

In the case of someone trying to convince you to join in an improper activity:

"Will you join us at that party tonight?"

"Why would you invite me to the party?"

"Are you afraid that if you get drunk with us you'll find out that you like it?"

"Why do you ask me that?"

"What is it with you? Do you think you're better than us?"

"Why would you ask me such a question?"

A person who is trying to put pressure on you will usually ask you a question. You feel obligated to answer, which puts you on the defensive. You are now doing battle on turf you never wanted to enter. The question "Why do you ask?" puts you back on your own ground. It changes the topic to the real issue, which is, why does this person feel he has the right to impose his concerns on you against your will? An uninvited question may be phrased politely, but it is really an aggressive attack on your integrity. The attack is all the more insidious because it takes advantage of your good nature, your unwillingness to rebuff a polite request. The response "Why do you ask?" is equally polite and equally forceful.

This response is quite effective in defending yourself from hearing gossip.

"Did you hear about what Jack did to Kara?"

"No, why do you ask?"

What can the person respond? "I just love to say bad things about people"?

A SELF-TEST

Below are some real-life situations. What is the best response to these situations, based on what you have learned in this book?

1. A friend of yours tells you that your "best friend" is saying behind your back that you are a nerd.

2. Your employer threatens to remember your disloyalty at promotion time unless you tell who you think has been goofing off on the job.

3. You never liked the kid who lives up the street. You see him go into the neighbor's house when they are out and come out with a television set.

4. You are in a car with some friends. They start gossiping about a person that you dislike.

5. Charlie has often hurt you by lying to you. A group of your friends is talking about how honest Charlie is. One of them is planning to buy Charlie's old car.

6. Yesterday you got carried away in a conversation and said nasty things about all of your friends.

7. You are uncomfortable with the conversation at a party and ask the others to change the subject. They look at you as if you have just landed from the moon.

8. You always thought that Mrs. Smith, your science teacher, was the best teacher in the school. Some of your friends are discussing the nominees for Teacher of the Year. Mrs. Smith is not among them.

9. You are in a group of people that are discussing politics. They ask your opinion of the President. You think that he is a lousy President.

10. People are always making fun of Doris because she is overweight. Someone asks you if Doris is a good cook (she is).

11. The Joneses are famous for barging in on people and imposing on them. They ask you if your friends the Dormats are hospitable. You know that they are.

12. Everyone is making fun of George because his parents did not come to the game to watch him play. George is crying but not saying anything. Yesterday he told you that his parents' business went bankrupt and they were too depressed to leave the house.

ESTABLISH A RITUAL TO FREE YOURSELF OF GOSSIP

Hopefully you are now inspired to observe the rules against gossip. You know that this will be difficult. The average person breaks these rules hundreds of times every day. There are numerous temptations to gossip, and many unclear situations. Do not imagine that you can cease gossiping altogether in one day. That would be too much to ask of yourself. Be patient, and do not take an all-or-nothing attitude. If you sincerely try, you will gradually learn to avoid gossip and to speak only good of others. It will be difficult at first, but the more you try, the easier it will become. Your acquaintances will learn that you do not like to hear gossip, and that will make your task much easier. You will notice the respect you get from others, and this will inspire you to keep trying.

Remember what the sages said: "Whatever path you choose, God will assist you. If you choose evil, God will help you to become evil. If you choose good, God will help you to become good." The sages also said that God says to us, "Give me an opening no larger than the eye of a needle, and I will open it for you so that wagons can drive through it" (Song of Songs Rabba 5:2). These sayings teach us that changing the way we speak of others is not as difficult as it may seem. We only have to make the original commitment. After that moment of decision a power beyond ourselves will help us to fulfill our resolution.

It may be that we can never completely free ourselves from gossip, but even if we learn to avoid gossip some of the time, that is still enough to make a difference in our lives. Every little improvement makes the world a better place.

Changing one's speech patterns requires daily attention, at least at the beginning. Read this book carefully and become familiar with its contents. Plan to read it again every six months or so in order to remember every detail. Use the summary at the end of this chapter as a daily checklist.

Review the list of rules every morning when you wake up. Tell yourself that you will try not to break any of these rules today. Take a few minutes to meditate on what your day will be like. Imagine the temptations to gossip that will arise and how you will overcome them. Pray for strength to resist the temptation to speak or listen to gossip. Now you are ready for the day.

At night, before you retire, think about the day that has passed. Consider each time you participated in gossip, and follow the three stages of repentance: Confess, express your regret, and resolve to do better in the future. Say a prayer of thanks for the times today that you were able to resist gossiping. Feel good about yourself and praise yourself for your moments of success.

After a few weeks or months of effort you will no longer need this twice-daily review. The rules for proper speech will be ingrained in your character. You will have progressed from knowledge to virtue. At that point you will only need an occasional review to keep yourself on the right track. Soon you will know the joy that comes from having only good things to say about others.

SUMMARY

1. Do not say anything about another person that will lower that person in the esteem of your listeners.

2. The fact that it is true does not make a derogatory statement about another person permissible. By definition, gossip is a true but derogatory statement. A false derogatory statement is slander.

3. Do not gossip even about a good friend. Your feelings about the subject and the feelings of the listeners are not relevant; what matters is the effect of the statement on the listeners.

4. Do not gratuitously disparage the possessions of another person, nor the goods of any merchant.

5. Even common knowledge should not be repeated if it is gossip.

6. Including yourself in a derogatory statement does not make it more acceptable. One should honor oneself as one honors others.

7. Disguising gossip as a joke or hinting at a derogatory meaning with irony and gestures does not decrease the negative effect of gossip.

8. Be as careful about gossip in writing as in speech. One should not show the written work of one person to another if it will cause embarrassment to the writer.

9. Do not listen to gossip. Whatever should not be said should also not be heard.

10. Make every effort to avoid hearing gossip, except when your intention is to correct the negative impressions it has created.

11. Resist engaging in gossip even at the risk of material loss or the loss of friends. This is a moral obligation.

12. People are judged by their deeds. In judging the deeds of others, ascribe the best possible motive to them. Judge all people to be righteous.

13. When making an ambiguous statement that could be taken as either praise or criticism, consider how your listeners will interpret your statement, and make it clear that your intention is to praise.

14. In discussing the actions of another person, be careful to use descriptive terms rather than judgmental terms.

15. Do not discuss the faulty character traits of another person, nor state that a person lacks a certain virtue, even a virtue that is rare.

16. Do not mention the past wrongs of a person who has repented.

17. You may make an example of a brazen wrongdoer, but exercise great caution in applying this description to anyone. This permission should never be used to discuss the misdeeds of someone whose actions have caused suffering to you personally.

18. Do not engage in talebearing—that is, telling one person what another person said about him or her.

19. You may transmit derogatory information about another person in order to save your listener from harm or material loss. But observe great caution in presenting a warning. Your intentions and the result of your words must be beneficial. (See the nine prerequisites in chapter 4.)

20. You may act upon a warning to protect yourself from harm, but do not accept a warning as fact or repeat it to others.

21. You may inquire about another person to protect yourself from possible harm or loss.

22. Answer truthfully to a request for a reference, but only to the extent that the information is relevant to the purposes of the one who inquires.

23. You may speak out against a person in order to recover a loss or protect yourself from harm.

24. Report crimes that have been or will be committed to the proper authorities. Report known instances of child abuse to the proper authorities. Do not inform against anyone to a tyrannical government whose interest is not justice but political persecution.

25. You may tell on children for their own benefit, if that is your sole intention. You may make an example of others to children for their moral instruction, following all proper precautions. You may prohibit your dependents and family members from associating with disreputable or dangerous persons.

26. Zeal for the truth is not a justification for gossip.

27. You are under no obligation to reveal the unknown misdeeds of others.

28. You may and should lie when telling the truth would create hard feelings and your sole intention is to create peace.

29. When asked to give an opinion, be honest if your opinion will have a beneficial effect on a future action or acquisition. Otherwise, say only nice things and try not to disagree with the one who asks.

30. Decline to give an opinion when you cannot be objective on account of a personal grudge or bad experience.

31. Never make an evaluative or judgmental comment about any group or class of people. Speak of all people as individuals.

32. Be particularly careful to avoid speaking or listening to ethnic, sexist, and racist humor.

33. You may discuss celebrities and public figures, but take care not to talk about them in a gossipy or slanderous manner. Avoid reading matter that discusses celebrities in an unethical way.

34. Your every word should have the force of a promise or solemn oath. Avoid taking oaths as much as possible, and treat all oaths with the highest regard.

35. Avoid the use of profanity in speech. To speak without profanity shows the greatest regard for your listeners, even if they are accustomed to such language.

36. When you are the victim of malicious gossip, hatred, or angry rebuke, refrain from responding in kind but accept the criticism with humility, trusting that no harm can come to you except as a result of your own actions.

37. You may deny having committed an immoral act. It is not necessary to respond to an unjust accusation beyond a simple denial.

38. Train oneself to accept rebuke.

39. Rebuke anyone who has wronged you. Speak the rebuke kindly, with the sole intention of righting the wrong and improving the perpetrator's deeds. Do not cause the subject of rebuke to blush or pale from shame.

40. Do not take personal revenge by words or deeds, but trust in divine justice. You may take a person to court for wrongs committed against yourself and may report crimes to the proper authorities. The judgment of a properly constituted court is an act of divine justice, not personal vengeance.

41. Hold your anger in until it has passed, then properly and kindly rebuke whoever caused you to become angry.

42. In a situation of verbal conflict with another person, have faith that you cannot be hurt by the other party's words, but

only by your own unkind and hurtful words. It is best to keep silent in the face of angry rebuke.

43. Treat every personal communication as a secret.

44. A public statement may be repeated to others, with certain precautions.

45. Be especially careful to keep secrets in conversations with your spouse or members of your household.

46. Do not divulge votes or statements that were made in a closed meeting.

47. You may reveal secrets to a professional advisor or clergyperson who is morally obligated to maintain your confidence.

48. When you have done wrong, always be ready to confess before God and before the victim of your misdeeds.

49. Be quick to forgive someone who has confessed and asked for forgiveness.

50. In repentance admit having done wrong, express regret for having done it, and vow not to repeat the wrong.

51. As an aspect of repentance, always try to undo the wrongs you have committed. While this is particularly difficult in the case of gossip, you should still do your best to undo the effects of your improperly spoken words.

52. Visit the sick, the bereaved, and the brokenhearted as often as possible. Speak words of consolation to them to the best of your ability.

53. Do not allow concern over what to say to prevent you from visiting those in need of consolation.